Dear Me, the Sky Is Falling

DEAR ME,
The Sky Is Falling

by

LEONARD SPIGELGASS

Based on a story by

GERTRUDE BERG &
JAMES YAFFE

Random House   New York

For
LAWRENCE LANGNER

***

But that doesn't say it at all—nor am I sure there *is* a way to say it, what I feel about Lawrence, what I know. And yet, I must try, for this play was his last production and so assumes a curiously undeserved historical place in the biography of a man who spanned the Broadway theatre from the twenties to the sixties and left as his distinctive, deeply engraved hallmark, The Theatre Guild Tudor Cottage. If you peer closely, you will see some of the greatest artists the world has ever known looking out of its windows.

I knew him since 1925; he did not know me until 1959. The way I knew him was that, as a young birthday present, I was given a subscription to The Theatre Guild each season. Opening-night seats—bad seats, but opening nights.

And those nights, agape, I'd watch the Establishment take their seats. Oh, I remember so well the Valentina and Chanel gowns, the Kilgour and French black ties, the fragrance of Patou's Joy, the ivory cigarette holders, and the scarab rings worn on the second finger of the left hand. Oh, those were the scarab years. And the great years of the theatre. Simultaneously, involved and apart, I was there.

So, I remember my association with The Guild, as an audience, not fragmentally but as whole memories. I even recall vividly it snowed on the night of the dress rehearsal of *Strange Interlude,* and rained on the night I saw *The Game of Love and Death.* I still see the faces of Claire Eames in *Ned McCobb's Daughter,* and Claudette Colbert in *Dynamo,* and Sterling Holloway singing "Manhattan," and Edith Meiser doing "Queen Elizabeth" in *The Garrick Gaieties,* and Edward G. Robinson in *The Brothers Karamazov,* and Miriam Hopkins in *The Camel Through the Needle's Eye,* and Romney Brent, and Tom Powers, and Betty Starbuck, and Glenn Anders, and Winifred Lenihan, and Nazimova, and above all, the Lunts—Lynn Fontanne and Alfred Lunt. What a fan I was—and am—and always will be.

A fan, too, of *Maximilian and Juarez* (or was it the other way around?), and *Mr. Pim,* and *Saint Joan,* and the incredible beauty of Margalo Gillmore in *Marco Millions,* and Dudley Digges—who could ever forget Dudley Digges?—and Alexander Kirkland as Francis Lightfoot in *Wings Over Europe,* and *Major Barbara,* too, and *The Devil's Disciple,* and *Caprice,* and *The Guardsman,* and *Idiot's Delight,* and *At Mrs. Beams.* . . .

But, as an English major, I was most impressed by the writing—the playwriting. Think of the authors Lawrence and his Theatre Guild exposed to me in performance: A. A. Milne, Ferenc Molnar, Leonid Andreyev, Bernard Shaw, Karl Capek, John Galsworthy, Ernest Toller, Marcel Pagnol, Franz Werfel, Sidney Howard, Luigi Pirandello, S. N. Behrman, Du Bose and Dorothy Heyward, Eugene O'Neill, Stefan Zweig, Ivan Turgenev, Philip Barry, Lynn Riggs, Robert E. Sherwood, Maxwell Anderson, Margaret Kennedy, Anton Chekov, William Saroyan,

DEAR ME, THE SKY IS FALLING

Tennessee Williams, Paul Osborn, Richard Rodgers and Oscar Hammerstein, George Kelly, Oscar Wilde, William Congreve, Terence Rattigan, John Van Druten, William Inge, John Patrick, Christopher Fry—and have I left out Shakespeare?

You can see from this list how Lawrence loved the beauty of the English language. It was a love that could only have been conceived in childhood, and in his autobiography, *The Magic Curtain*, he gives a large share of credit to his mother.

He was born in the town of Swansea in South Wales, on May 30, 1890—and, with only two years of boarding school, at thirteen he was turned out into the world to earn his own living. There were two advertisements in the London *Daily Telegraph:*

The first one read:
> Junior Clerk Wanted:
> Excellent opportunity for ambitious young man, apply Jay's, Oxford Circus.

The second one read:
> Junior Clerk Wanted:
> Theatrical business. Apply in person.
> J. Bannister Howard, 3 Bedford Street, Strand.

He showed both advertisements to his mother, who advised that he call at Jay's first. The Messrs. Jay insulted Lawrence's pride by agreeing to hire him as an office boy and then permitting him to work later in the ladies' stocking department. Office boy, indeed! Ladies' stockings, pfah!

Indignant, he proceeded immediately to 3 Bedford Street, Strand, where there hung a large sign bearing the legend: The Ben Greet Academy of Acting. He was engaged by Mr. J. Bannister Howard at a salary of eight shillings a week. Mr. Howard shared his suite of offices with other theatrical managers, one of whom was a Mr. William Courtney, manager for Ellen Terry.

I'm afraid he paid very little attention to Mr. Howard's business but rather devoted himself to Mr. Courtney and Miss Terry, who was rehearsing the role of Portia in *The Merchant of Venice*. On her opening night, in the tumble-down old Camden Town Theatre, Lawrence saw Miss Terry—and thereafter he was forever the theatre's slave.

He lasted at 3 Bedford Street for three years until, at his mother's economic urging, he became a chartered patent agent at 3 Chancery Lane, the London office of the firm of Cruikshank and Fairweather.

So began the extraordinary split in his personality—one compartment labeled "art"—the other compartment labeled "business."

It continued all the years he lived.

On the one hand, he distinguished himself as a member of America's leading firm of patent attorneys and initiated the National Inventors Council, which contributed so brilliantly to the war effort. On the other hand, he engaged actively in the writing and production of plays. With Edward Goodman, Philip Moeller, Helen Westley, Josephine A. Meyer, Lucy Huffaker, Ida Rauh, Dudley Tucker, and Albert Boni, he founded the Washington Square Players in 1914.

In 1918, with Philip Moeller, Theresa Helburn, Lee Simonson, Rollo Peters, and Maurice Wertheim, he founded The Theatre Guild. In his book, he tells why.

"I had faith in the desire of a large section of the American public for better things in the theatre, and I wished to test whether my faith was justified. To this extent there was involved in the formation of The Theatre Guild a crusading spirit which made what we were doing more exciting than the mere producing of plays as a matter of self-expression or profit."

But profit there was in the forty-five years in which Lawrence headed The Guild. Profit and loss, and heartache, and disaster, and triumph—and always plans and more plans for the future.

The Theatre Guild subscription system, whereby audiences bought their tickets for a series of plays was his idea, and later he conceived its national offspring, The American Theatre Society. The Westport Country Playhouse that brought a new dimension to summer theatre also came from Lawrence. Then, the absurd notion of having a Shakespeare theatre in the United States, Langner's Folly, turned into the American Shakespeare Festival Theatre at Stratford, Connecticut. For many seasons, now, it has presented the best American actors, directors, and scenic designers in an extraordinary collection of Shakespearian comedies, tragedies, and histories. Without Lawrence, it would not have existed.

While continuing to produce plays in New York, in collaboration with his wife, Armina Marshall, and his son, Philip, he still took an active interest in his patent firm and found time to write for the *New York Times,* and *Saturday Review,* and, of course, many books on the theatre, on clothes, and on playwriting.

Yet, to see him at his home in Westport, supervising the planting of the bulbs, or making major decisions about his apple orchards, or simply telling stories to his two grandchildren, you would have thought he was a man of leisure. His secret, I think, was that those two compartments in his life were in themselves compartmentalized—and that he could, by processes unknown to less intelligent men, concentrate on one problem until it was solved, and then turn to the other, without letting one worry bleed into the other.

In the summer of 1960, when he was a most reluctant seventy, he came to the Coast, wearing yellow pants and a Balinese sport shirt, a crinkled linen jacket, and a Panama hat—a thoroughly ridiculous outfit which became him and made him look more dignified than ever. We sat in the garden and he laughed when I ranted, as I've just been ranting, and he told me of the agonies and the ecstasies of The Guild.

And he told me though he didn't mean to—of his unique perseverance, and he said that if you wanted a word for him, *stage-struck* would do as well as any.

As he talked of the future, I knew he was *still* stage-struck and still making plans: An extension of the sub-scription program in the United States, an Academy and School of Acting for the Shakespeare Theatre in Stratford, Connecticut, a heating system for Westport to increase its season and enable it to do repertory, a vision of a multi-religious shrine of theatre, ballet, poetry, and art in Jeru-salem, three new plays—no, four new plays—a book on Shaw, a book on O'Neill—and suddenly he dozed, the way he always did towards the end. But I don't think it was dozing; I think it was dreaming.

L.S.

DEAR ME, THE SKY IS FALLING *was first presented by The Theatre Guild at The Music Box, New York City, on March 2, 1963, with the following cast:*

(IN ORDER OF APPEARANCE)

DR. ROBERT EVANS	William Daniels
DEBBIE HIRSCH	Jill Kraft
LIBBY HIRSCH	Gertrude Berg
MILDRED	Tresa Hughes
PAUL HIRSCH	Howard da Silva
SOPHIE	Mimi Randolph
JESSIE	Sylvia Mann
MINNIE	Minerva Pious
ROBERT WOLFE	Michael Baseleon
MR. SCHLINGER	Carl Don
MRS. SCHLINGER	Martha Greenhouse
PETER NEMO	Ron Leibman

Directed by Herman Shumlin
Settings and lighting by Will Steven Armstrong
Costumes by Edith Lutyens Bel Geddes

SYNOPSIS OF SCENES

Act One

ACT ONE

The scene: DR. ROBERT EVANS' *office. It is equipped with normal furniture—not of the clinical variety. To one side of the door is a black leather couch. To the other side is* DR. EVANS' *desk and a swivel chair. A second swivel chair is nearby. On the walls are the usual diplomas and a few pictures. It is an afternoon in April.*

At rise: DR. EVANS, *Anglo-Saxon, thirty-five, is seated at his desk. A buzzer sounds. He pushes a button and picks up the phone.*

DOCTOR   Yes? . . . Have her come right in.
(*He rises and opens the door, admitting* DEBBIE HIRSCH, *an attractive young woman of twenty-five*)

DEBBIE   Dr. Evans?

DOCTOR   Yes.

DEBBIE (*As they shake hands*)   I'm Deborah Hirsch.

DOCTOR   Yes, I know.
(*She moves inside. He closes the door*)

DEBBIE   My aunt Mildred says you are a very good psychoanalyst and that you can help me.

DOCTOR   I'll be very glad to try. Sit down. (*She sits in a swivel chair. He sits at his desk*)   Now, what is it you want to tell me?

DEBBIE (*Genuinely upset*)   I have a small problem, Doc-

3

tor. I'm not entirely sure how deep. It's been worrying me terribly—so much so that I'm becoming neurotic—or psychotic—I'm not quite sure of the difference.

DOCTOR   The cliché distinction is: A psychotic knows that two and two are *five*. A neurotic knows that two and two are *four*—but worries about it.

DEBBIE (*More at ease*) Well, I certainly worried about coming here, Doctor—so I guess that qualifies me as a full-fledged neurotic.

DOCTOR   Not necessarily. It's perfectly normal to have some tension on your first visit.

DEBBIE Thank you. That helps. Where shall I begin, Doctor?

DOCTOR   Where would you like to begin, Miss Hirsch?

DEBBIE I thought at the beginning. Do you think that's wise?

DOCTOR   If you do.

DEBBIE Well, here I go. I was premature—not quite seven months—born in the Post—(*Interrupting herself*) Aren't I supposed to lie down?

DOCTOR   Well, it's up to you, Miss Hirsch.

DEBBIE I'd rather, please. I want to do this right.

DOCTOR (*Rising as she does*) Certainly, Miss Hirsch.
(*She places her coat on the swivel chair, goes to the couch and lies down, holding her small purse and gloves. As she begins to talk, the* DOCTOR *takes his clipboard from the desk and moves his chair to sit behind her*)

DEAR ME, THE SKY IS FALLING

DEBBIE I was premature—not quite seven months—born in the Post Graduate Hospital just about the time of Munich, to put me in historical perspective. I got my degree at Barnard. Currently, I'm an assistant editor at Doubleday in Children's Books. Simultaneously, I am writing my own rather *formless* novel, which I haven't dared show to a publisher yet. . . . I live at home in New Rochelle. My father's in the belt business—and he's an ally. I mean, he's understanding.

DOCTOR I'm glad to hear it.

DEBBIE I have two sisters, Clara and Louise, and one brother, Theodore. They all live away from New York —Chicago, Los Angeles and Los Alamos. I have nine assorted nieces and nephews—lots of aunts and uncles and dozens of cousins and—well, that's my full spectrum.

DOCTOR You haven't mentioned your mother.

DEBBIE Oh, I must have.

DOCTOR Do you often ignore her?

DEBBIE Nobody ignores my mother!

DOCTOR Oh?

DEBBIE She's a perfectly normal woman—astute, cheerful, perennially possessive. We've a good solid relationship—as long as she keeps her nose out of my business.

DOCTOR And when she doesn't?

DEBBIE I could just kill her! Oh, I don't mean that literally of course. I mean, I have average resentments, but then everybody does. These days, we all know what mothers are, don't we, Doctor? Momism and that sort of thing. Philip Wylie, you know.

5

DEAR ME, THE SKY IS FALLING

DOCTOR   Is Philip Wylie your problem?

DEBBIE   No. And neither is momism! My mother is not the reason I've come to see you! I can handle her—if I have to—and I don't have to very much.

DOCTOR   How much is "not very much," Miss Hirsch?

DEBBIE   It's in the little things we have the most trouble —shoes, for instance, and clothes. She is forever going to town and picking things out for me and I am forever sending them back.

DOCTOR   Does that make you feel triumphant, Miss Hirsch?

DEBBIE   It isn't a question of feeling triumphant. Doctor, I do wish we'd get to my problem.

DOCTOR   What is your problem, Miss Hirsch?

DEBBIE   My problem, Doctor, is equated with my fiancé. From the very first moment I saw him, I found him enormously attractive—in sexual terms. He's an attorney —Yale Law School—junior partner in McNeal, McNeal, Lawson and Bowle, Twenty-three Broadway. Really extraordinary the far road he's traveled from Sheepshead Bay to Turtle Bay.

DOCTOR   What's your fiancé's name?

DEBBIE   Well, Doctor, *that's* the reason I've come to see you. Because—well—I don't know his name—I mean, I can't remember!

DOCTOR   At the moment or for some time?

DEBBIE   Almost from the beginning. I have to write it down. (*Opening her purse and removing a slip of pa-*

per) Robert Wolfe! A pleasant name and not uncommon. I don't see why I should have such trouble remembering it. . . . It worried me terribly, so I dug out my copy of *The Basic Writings of Sigmund Freud,* and I flipped when I found his very *first* chapter deals with the forgetting of names. It was that that made me realize I had to have help—because it appears there's an underlying psychic mechanism that takes hold—

DOCTOR Do you think we're quite ready for psychic mechanisms?

DEBBIE Well, I hope we will be soon, because this is April and the wedding is in June! . . . Oh, the full horror at the Hampshire House. . . . If it could all just disappear! The wedding of Miss Deborah Hirsch to Mr. Peter Nemo.

DOCTOR Who is Peter Nemo?

DEBBIE Peter Nemo? How did he get into this?

DOCTOR You just mentioned him.

DEBBIE I did?! I'd rather not go on about him.

DOCTOR Why not?

DEBBIE Ohhh, he's just a boy I used to know—a raggle-taggle poet. I've outgrown him. He was in my Greenwich Village or Blue Period. He fragmented me. His hatred of possessions and his desire to possess. It used to tear me to pieces.

DOCTOR Does it still?

DEBBIE No. It's finished. And now there's Robert— Oh, I'm so relieved! I do remember his name!

DOCTOR Yes . . . ?

DEAR ME, THE SKY IS FALLING

DEBBIE   It's Robert!

DOCTOR   Yes?

DEBBIE   Robert Evans!

DOCTOR   That's *my* name, Miss Hirsch.

Curtain

The scene: The living room of the Hirsch home in New Rochelle. It is clean, comfortable and well-furnished in traditional reproductions. At one side of the front door is a grand piano, to the other side, a sunroom. Adjacent to the sunroom is a swinging door leading to a pantry. Beyond the pantry is a dining area. A stairway leads to the upper rooms. Near the foot of the stairs is a table with two chairs. Several boxes of Tiffany wedding invitations are on the table. A number of wedding gifts are on display—some packages opened, others unopened. It is a Thursday evening, three weeks later.

At rise: LIBBY HIRSCH *is on the stage alone, talking on the telephone.*

LIBBY I'm in a quandary, darling, about the wedding menu. I can't decide whether it should be mock turtle soup or fresh fruit supreme to start. Then, I thought maybe sirloin of beef with potatoes Anna . . . and little French peas . . . and asparagus with hollandaise sauce because Robert loves them. Then a salad—endive—and, for dessert, sherbet and wedding cake. And, of course, wines and salted nuts and peppermints. . . . Simple but filling. . . . Yeah . . . Uh-huh . . . Are you sure you want to bother with a party for Debbie now? (MIL-DRED *comes from the dining room with wedding-invitation envelopes. She is in her late forties, still very attractive, prim and well coiffured, slightly lined around the mouth, and has the mien of a school teacher. To* MILDRED) Did you find the envelopes, Mildred?

9

MILDRED   Yes, Libby, I did.

> (*She sits at the table and begins addressing envelopes*)

LIBBY (*Back to the phone*)   I was talking to my sister. She's helping with the invitations. Well, if you're thinking of a party, may I suggest a miscellaneous shower? . . . I'll let you know about the date. . . . You're so sweet to suggest it. . . . Well, this is my last wedding. . . . I'm exhausted, but—you know something? I love it. . . . How would you know with four boys? . . . All right, darling, I'll let you know later about the date. . . . Right. Bye. (*She hangs up, then to* MILDRED) Have you many more invitations to do?

MILDRED   I'm almost finished with our side. Robert's list I haven't even started.

LIBBY   Very impressive, huh? Four judges and two congressmen.

PAUL (*Enters, coming downstairs. He's an attractive man in his mid-fifties, conservatively tailored in Brooks Brothers fashion, efficient and successful in business, loyal and dedicated to his family*)   Not even *one* senator?

LIBBY (*To* MILDRED)   Look under J.

MILDRED   You think Senator Javits will come?

LIBBY   He'll come.

PAUL   I better order a new dinner jacket.
> (*He looks over some brochures and blueprints on houses in Florida*)

LIBBY   You're stunning in white tie.

PAUL   Black tie.

LIBBY   We'll see.

DEAR ME, THE SKY IS FALLING

PAUL We've seen. Black tie.

LIBBY (*Going to the table where* MILDRED *is working*) I'll help you with the invitations, darling.

PAUL You got a canasta game tonight, Libby.

LIBBY Look how I forgot! How am I going to put my head on canasta tonight? Paul, darling, put up the bridge table, please?

PAUL Where do you keep the bridge table?

LIBBY What's the matter, you don't live here? I'll get it.

PAUL In Florida, we'll have a permanent game room. We are going to *enjoy* life!

LIBBY I'm enjoying life. My cup runneth over. (*Looks at her watch*) It would run over a little bit more if I knew where my youngest daughter was.
   (PAUL *and* MILDRED *exchange a look*)

PAUL She told you. She went to the dentist.

LIBBY Why she has to go to a dentist in New York, I'll never know. Paul, what did I do with that bridge table?

PAUL What's the matter, you don't live here? (LIBBY *smiles and starts toward the dining room*) Come here, Libby. I want to show you something. Best of all, I like these houses Joe Weldon is building in Florida.
   (*He shows her a photo*)

LIBBY We'll discuss Florida after the wedding. And, besides, what happens to your business?

PAUL I've been negotiating with Charlie Finkel to buy me out.

LIBBY It would be better if you bought him out.

PAUL Libby, how many times do I have to say it? We started out two. We became six. Now, we're almost two again. . . . Why do we need to rattle around in a ten-room house? Why do I have to wait for the eight-o-three —and shovel snow—and put up storm windows?

LIBBY You sound like a senior citizen.

PAUL I sound like a man who's divesting himself of unnecessary problems. I sound like a man who's planned and earned a decent retirement.

LIBBY Retirement means more than sitting in a golf wagon. With nothing to do, time can be very heavy.

PAUL (*Swinging an imaginary club*) I'll be on the first tee every morning, at eight sharp.

LIBBY Yeah, and while you're on the first tee, what will I be doing?

MILDRED You could caddy for him.

LIBBY All of a sudden, everybody's pushing me outdoors. I like the indoors.

PAUL Libby, I'd like to put down a deposit.

LIBBY And if you sell your business, what happens to your help? You have a responsibility. Take, for instance, a woman like Selma Harris—she's been working for you for fifteen years—

PAUL Miss Harris hasn't worked for me for six months.

LIBBY You didn't tell me.

PAUL What was there to tell?

LIBBY (*To* MILDRED) See if Selma Harris is on the list. Look under H.

PAUL   I don't want Selma Harris at the wedding.

LIBBY   Give me one good reason why Selma shouldn't be invited to the wedding.

PAUL   The subject is closed.
(*He goes upstairs*)

LIBBY   So we'll re-open it. (*To* MILDRED) Put Selma Harris on the list.

MILDRED   (*Looks to see that* PAUL *is out of sight*) Libby, if I were you, I wouldn't press the Selma Harris matter.

LIBBY   Don't make a mountain, like you always did when you were adolescent.

MILDRED   My problem is—I was a sibling.

LIBBY   What's a sibling?

MILDRED   If there are two children in a family—one is a sibling.

LIBBY   Which one?

MILDRED   The other one.

LIBBY   That's just as clear as all your explanations about psychiatry.

MILDRED   Libby, don't be so patronizing. It did me a lot of good.

LIBBY   The only good I can see is you had your nose fixed.

MILDRED   It was a deviated septum.

LIBBY   Oh, that's what it was! Thank you very much. (*Taking an address card from one of the file boxes and handing it to* MILDRED) Mildred, send an invitation to your David. It'll be a good way to get together again.

MILDRED (*Tearing up the card*) No. I'm perfectly contented being separated. I'm adjusted to my life the way it is, and that's maturity.

LIBBY Some maturity. Teaching school all day and going home to an empty apartment at night. You deserve a little more out of life.

MILDRED Libby, please don't interfere.

LIBBY I'm not interfering.
(*The front door opens and* DEBBIE *enters, happy and gay.* LIBBY *rises*)

DEBBIE Hi, Mama!

LIBBY Hi!

DEBBIE Hi, Aunt Mildred! It's a lovely night out. I walked from the station.

LIBBY Let me look at you! When you're in a good mood, you're even prettier! So how's your malocclusion?

DEBBIE It's going to be a long job.

LIBBY Tell me, what's his name, your fancy dentist?

DEBBIE Dr. Evans. Anybody call?

LIBBY Anybody? Everybody! And Mrs. Kaplan wants to make you a miscellaneous shower.

DEBBIE Oh, no. Just too many showers and too many dinners and I'm rocky.

LIBBY You're not rocky. I think you're hungry. I kept you warm on the stove. Come have a bite.

DEBBIE What have you got?

LIBBY Cutlets.

DEBBIE Ohhhh, no.

LIBBY You don't want cutlets, I'll make you a hamburger.

DEBBIE Maybe some French toast!

LIBBY (*Having the last word*) With loganberry syrup! (*To* MILDRED) Maybe my sibling sister would like to have something? (*As she goes through the pantry door, chuckling*) Sibling! A new word!

DEBBIE How did she ever get to know a word like sibling?

MILDRED It popped out of me and she picked it right up. I wouldn't be a bit surprised if she suspects something.

DEBBIE Not Mama. She never holds back.

MILDRED (*Eagerly*) How was it today? Are you on a plateau?

(PAUL *starts downstairs*)

DEBBIE (*Seeing him*) Hi ya, Pop!

PAUL Hi, Baby. How can she be on a plateau after only three weeks?

DEBBIE It was a shattering session. I said the most terrible things—and he said even worse things back to me. But the paradox is—instead of being depressed, I'm elated!

MILDRED Euphoria.

PAUL What's euphoria?

MILDRED False happiness.

PAUL If she's happy, why does it have to be false?

MILDRED It has something to do with her id.

PAUL Who's the analyst—you or Dr. Evans?

MILDRED I'm analytically oriented.

DEBBIE Maybe I'm beginning to be. I don't feel so crushed.

PAUL Baby, I wish I understood what was crushing you.

MILDRED Aren't you glad I suggested him?

DEBBIE I love you, Aunt Mildred. You're my friend.

MILDRED Remember—if anything ever goes wrong and you need an oasis, I still have that extra bedroom.

DEBBIE I'm not going to need it.
(*She kisses* MILDRED *and starts upstairs. The phone rings and she comes back down as* PAUL *picks it up.* LIBBY *comes from the pantry*)

PAUL Hello. . . . Hello, how are you, my boy? . . . How did it go in court today? . . . Fine.

LIBBY Let me talk to him.

PAUL (*Handing phone to* DEBBIE) It's your future.

LIBBY Just one minute, Debbie?

DEBBIE (*Smiles, giving her the phone*) Just one minute, Mama.
(*She sits on the second step.* PAUL *goes to the sunroom for his putter*)

LIBBY (*Into the phone*) Hello, Sonny! . . . Please excuse me for jumping on the phone, but I want your advice. . . . Well, it's between mock turtle soup and fresh fruit supreme to start. . . . Well, we couldn't have real turtle because most of my guests wouldn't eat it—including me. So we'll settle for fresh fruit. Goodbye.
(*She almost hangs up*)

DEBBIE Mama!

LIBBY (*Into the phone*) Oh, excuse me! Here's Debbie. (*To* DEBBIE) I'm sorry, Debbie.
> (*She hands the phone to* DEBBIE. PAUL, *with a golf club, putts an imaginary ball*)

DEBBIE (*Into the phone*) Hi. . . . What am I doing? I'm talking to you. . . . Then I'm going upstairs and take a bath. . . .

LIBBY (*Sitting on the telephone bench, with delighted interest*) I bought you some new bubble stuff—

DEBBIE Then I'm going to get dressed and wait for you.

LIBBY Tell Sonny—in addition to the seven-piece orchestra, there'll be a small combo—no brass.

MILDRED Are you spending money!

LIBBY How many times does a girl get married?

DEBBIE (*Covering the phone*) Three . . . four . . .

LIBBY Bite your tongue.

DEBBIE (*Into the phone*) Yes . . . Yes . . .

LIBBY Tell Sonny I just happened to be passing a travel agency today—

DEBBIE I'll be ready—

LIBBY And I have a wonderful idea for your honeymoon—

DEBBIE There's that Swedish movie I've been wanting to see—

LIBBY Tell him Lake Louise and Banff—

PAUL *Please!* Don't disturb her, Libby.

LIBBY Who's disturbing her?

DEBBIE No, I'd really rather see the Swedish movie.

LIBBY You and Sonny can get a private cottage with a balcony overlooking the lake.

PAUL Libby, please! She's talking!

DEBBIE I'll be ready. Goodbye.
(*She hands the phone to* LIBBY)

LIBBY Bye, Sonny! (*She hangs up*) Lake Louise and Banff are beautiful.

DEBBIE Mama, I very much appreciate your ideas about Lake Louise and Banff, but I really want to go to Europe.

LIBBY If I thought you'd made up your mind, I wouldn't have mentioned it.

DEBBIE We've decided. (*She turns to stairs, then back*) And, Mama, could you do me a favor I'd really appreciate?

LIBBY Anything, darling.

DEBBIE Could you please stop calling him Sonny?

LIBBY You know why I do it? It's crazy, but all of a sudden, sometimes I can't remember his name.
(DEBBIE *stares, emits a small moan and runs upstairs.* PAUL *quickly follows* DEBBIE, *gesturing that he will handle the situation*)

LIBBY She's changeable like the wind lately.

MILDRED Who can blame her? You're making the honeymoon plans.

LIBBY I thought if they went to a quiet place, she could get to know him a little better.

MILDRED *After* they're married?

LIBBY Millie, you know I didn't mean that.

MILDRED   You're trying to make her too dependent on you.

LIBBY   So now she'll have a husband to depend on.

MILDRED   You fixed that.

LIBBY   What's the meaning of that remark?

MILDRED   You took her to Westhampton. You were afraid she was going to be an old maid.

LIBBY   *I* was worried my Debbie was going to be an old maid? Well, thank God, she'll have a marvelous life. Robert's a fine boy with a brilliant future.

MILDRED   Also a past. With a married woman. Libby, everybody knows it.

LIBBY   Certainly he knew other girls before he knew Debbie. What young man doesn't? But that's all over.

MILDRED   According to whom is it all over, for instance?

LIBBY   According to his mother, for instance.

MILDRED   You and his mother—a regular secret service.

LIBBY   We never even lifted a finger.

MILDRED   The same way with all your children you never lifted a finger.
       (*She takes her purse from the table and opens it, removes her gloves*)

LIBBY   Yes, I lifted a finger! Not one. I lifted ten fingers! One finger for my children's education. Another finger so they—

MILDRED   I've heard that already!

LIBBY   And my door was always open for my children's friends. And out there for twenty-five years there's a welcome mat—

MILDRED   It didn't say such a big welcome to Peter Nemo.

LIBBY   Peter Nemo? A forgotten incident.

MILDRED   That's what you think. I personally happen to know she still has regrets on that subject.
(PAUL *comes downstairs with the card table*)

LIBBY   If she did, she'd have told me. My Debbie tells me everything.

MILDRED   There are some things a daughter can't tell a mother.

LIBBY   Please, Millie, stop before I say something!

MILDRED   For instance, I suppose you'll say, because I've never been a mother I don't understand about these things!

LIBBY   If the shoe fits—

MILDRED   Thank you for a lovely evening!

LIBBY   I apologize for what I didn't say.

MILDRED   You never talk so loud as when you don't say it.
(*She is putting on her gloves*)

LIBBY   You always jump off the handle! It was always the same with Mama. You always had to have the last word! You always had to have the punctuation mark—slamming the door. . . . There's the door—slam it!

MILDRED (*Opening the door*)   I will!
(*She does.* LIBBY *opens the door and calls after her*)

LIBBY   Will you be here for supper tomorrow night?

MILDRED (*Offstage*)   Certainly! . . . I still have a hundred more envelopes to do.
(PAUL *places the card table near the sofa*)

DEAR ME, THE SKY IS FALLING

LIBBY (*Closing the door*) Oh, that Millie!

PAUL Libby, you shouldn't have made that remark.

LIBBY I know. But she always upsets me so. How's Debbie?

PAUL Debbie is also upset.

LIBBY If she is, it's perfectly natural. Every girl, before she gets married, begins to debate. Is it right? Is it wrong? He loves me. He loves me not. . . . Paul, you think she loves him, no?

PAUL I don't know about love; I'm too old.

LIBBY Since when are you all of a sudden so old, Paul?

PAUL Since when? Since we have the first President who's younger than I am.

LIBBY To me, you're younger than springtime. I'm as romantic about Debbie's wedding as I was about my own.

PAUL Except now you have nine grandchildren.

LIBBY And do I ever see them? For children I have Arabs. (*The doorbell rings*) See who it is, darling.

PAUL (*Looks out the door, turns back*) The canasta ladies! Please! Don't open the door until I get out of here! (*He gets a golf club from the bag in the sunroom*)

LIBBY Remember when there were eight of us and we had two tables of bridge?

PAUL Every time they walk in, I realize I'm the only husband left and I begin to get symptoms!

LIBBY (*At the door*) Don't get symptoms, because I'll never talk to you again!

PAUL Don't worry, sweetheart! In Florida, we'll live to be

a hundred and nine. I'll be in the garage having a little putting practice.

(*He disappears through the pantry door as* LIBBY *admits* SOPHIE, JESSIE *and* MINNIE. *They are about* LIBBY'S *age*)

SOPHIE   Here we are!

MINNIE   Hello!

JESSIE   Hello! How are you!?

LIBBY (*Taking* JESSIE'S *coat*)   I'll take your coats.

JESSIE   Wait! I'll get my Kleenex!
(*She retrieves it from her coat pocket*)

SOPHIE   Oh, you're doing marvelous! Even before the invitations are out!

LIBBY   Listen, we didn't keep the wedding exactly a secret.

SOPHIE   Everything's on display, just like they do in the movies! That's stunning! (*She picks up a silver candelabrum*)   Is this sterling or plated?

LIBBY   Antique Sheffield.

MINNIE   Do you think young people appreciate silver these days? You have to take a day off to clean it.

LIBBY   They can afford help.

SOPHIE (*Taking a napkin from a gift box on the end of the telephone bench*)   Ohhh . . . This is a beautiful luncheon set.

LIBBY (*Proudly*)   From my corsetiere!

JESSIE   Miss Schneider!

SOPHIE   She makes my brassieres, too.

DEAR ME, THE SKY IS FALLING

JESSIE   Is it linen?

SOPHIE   Real linen?

LIBBY   Pure.

MINNIE (*Placing a moistened forefinger under a corner of the napkin*)   Pure.

LIBBY (*Having the last word*)   Twenty-four napkins.

MINNIE   Is it true you're moving to Florida?

LIBBY   Florida? Who's running to Florida? Especially now when my Debbie needs me the most.

MINNIE   If my Natalie was married, I'd run.

LIBBY   The right man will come along.

MINNIE   He's certainly taking his time.

LIBBY   Tell me, did your Natalie lose any more weight?

MINNIE   Since she's going to the psychiatrist, she's lost twenty-six pounds.

LIBBY   She could have lost the twenty-six pounds without psychiatry. A new business! Once my Debbie is married, I'll concentrate on your Natalie. (*She goes to the pantry door, then calls upstairs*)   Debbie, darling, I pressed your navy-blue suit. I thought you might like to wear it tonight. (*To the girls*)   I'll get some fruit so we can nibble.

> (LIBBY *goes into the pantry. The ladies sit at the card table*)

JESSIE (*Fanning out cards on the table, face down*)   Girls, are we playing for a twentieth?

SOPHIE   Fine with me.

> (*As they draw cards,* MINNIE *extends a wrist heavy with a charm bracelet*)

MINNIE Look—from my fourth grandchild. The twins
. . . from Jerry . . . from Ava.
(*As they exclaim over the new charm,* LIBBY *comes
from the pantry with a bowl of fruit, fruit plates
and napkins and places them on the coffee table.
Then she goes off into the dining room*)

JESSIE (*Gathering up the cards*) It comes out Libby and
me against Minnie and you, Sophie.

MINNIE Oh, Sophie, change places with me, please. The
light is bad for my eyes. (SOPHIE *rises and they shift
seats clockwise*) Thank you.

SOPHIE I don't mind. I'm wearing my contact lenses.

JESSIE (*Dealing furiously*) Libby, will you stop fussing
and sit down?

LIBBY (*Coming from the dining room with a box of ciga-
rettes, matches and ash trays*) How I'm going to put
my head on canasta I don't know.
(*She sits*)

JESSIE Are we playing or not?

LIBBY I'm playing! I'm playing! Let's see what I've got
here.
(*They arrange their cards industriously.* LIBBY
hums)

MINNIE (*Suddenly, slapping her cards on the table*)
Ohhh!   I'll kill myself!

SOPHIE I've got a hand like a foot!

LIBBY (*She almost sings it*) I'm perfectly contented!
(*She suddenly rises, putting her cards on the table*)
There's our Sonny! Never a minute late! Never!

SOPHIE Who hears the doorbell?

LIBBY   I can hear the engine of his Jaguar XKE when he turns the corner. (*She calls towards the stairs*)   Debbie! Your fiancé is here!

> (*She opens the door, admitting* ROBERT WOLFE. *He is in his thirties, handsome, well tailored, full of self-confidence. He carries two small bunches of violets*)

ROBERT   Hi!

LIBBY   Come in, son-in-law minus three weeks! Debbie'll be right down.

ROBERT   (*Handing her a bunch of violets*)   There's a boy working his way through college selling two bunches for the price of one.

LIBBY   How thoughtful—the exact color of my wedding dress—periwinkle. I'll put them in the icebox.

ROBERT   No, wear them.

LIBBY   I should wear a corsage to play canasta?

ROBERT   Good evening, ladies. I'm sorry. I should have gotten one for each of you. (*They ad lib replies*)   Winning or losing?

LIBBY   We just began, but Jessie'll win. She always does.

JESSIE   I cheat!
> (*They laugh*)

LIBBY   Can I fix you something?

ROBERT   No, thanks. I've just had a seven-course banquet. Want to hear the menu?

LIBBY   I know your mother's menus.

ROBERT   Debbie and I will have to live on Metrecal.

LIBBY Don't worry about Debbie. She's not such a fancy cook.

ROBERT Any more secrets I ought to know, Mrs. Hirsch?

LIBBY My Debbie is an open book.

SOPHIE Aren't you going to look at all the loot?

LIBBY (*Laughs*) Loot!

ROBERT How many fruit knives, candlesticks and electric percolators?

LIBBY Mr. McNeal sent you a Picasso—

SOPHIE A lithograph—

LIBBY *Signed!* . . . And the other Mr. McNeal sent you a beautiful silver dish— And over there's a beautiful luncheon set.

SOPHIE They'll need service plates.

LIBBY They got service plates—from you, Sophie.

SOPHIE I wondered if they came. . . . (LIBBY *points to a box on the other side of the room.* ROBERT *goes to the box and takes a plate out*) They're Limoges and *I* got them as a wedding present. But what do I do with service plates in two and a half rooms?

ROBERT (*Admiring the plate*) These are beautiful porcelain. Thank you, Mrs. Radin.
        (*Returns the plate to its box*)

SOPHIE Call me Aunt Sophie. All of us are honorary aunts in this family.

ROBERT Okay—Aunt Sophie, Aunt Jessie and Aunt Minnie. It's quite a haul. If we ever go broke, we can hock everything. (*He looks into an A&P box under a table, taking out the gift card enclosed*) What's this?

LIBBY (*Uneasy*) Don't even bother looking at that.
(DEBBIE *comes downstairs*, not *wearing the navy-blue suit*)

MINNIE Look at that vision. What I wouldn't do for that waistline.

SOPHIE I had it and look what I did with it.
(ROBERT *and* DEBBIE *embrace at the foot of the stairs*)

LIBBY Did you ever see such a handsome couple?

DEBBIE (*To the girls, looking over her shoulder*) Hello, everybody! (ROBERT, *his arms still around her, holds the violets up behind her shoulder so she sees them. She takes them*) Oh, I love violets.

LIBBY I also got.

ROBERT (*Indicating the gifts*) And we also got. I've just been examining the pillage and plunder, Debbie. Where are we going to put it all?
(*He moves to the A&P carton, bending over it*)

DEBBIE Mama's the dish-closet expert.

ROBERT (*Opening the box and pulling the enclosed mobile partly out*) I'm not too sure about this, though.

LIBBY Forget that.

ROBERT It's a mess of pin wheels.
(*Puts it back in the box and looks at the card*)

LIBBY Wouldn't go with Regency.

DEBBIE (*Interested, looks in the box*) It's a mobile. Who sent *that*?

ROBERT (*Reading the card*) "Watch this as it violates space—and annihilates time—and reminds you of a roseate world, now chinchilla gray, whirling in the despair

of an affluent society." It's in purple ink, no signature.
(*As he reads,* DEBBIE *has straightened up and stared stonily at her violets*)

DEBBIE   The signature is built in! Only one man could have written that!

LIBBY (*To* ROBERT)   Peter Nemo. A boy Debbie went to school with.

SOPHIE   I remember him. He always was a little nutty.

LIBBY   She hasn't seen him in years.

DEBBIE   Don't discuss it, Mama! Just send it back.

ROBERT   That wouldn't be very nice, Debbie.

DEBBIE (*Angrily*)   It's arrogant, Robert, and I don't want it!

ROBERT   Okay. Don't bite my head off. Anything you say.

LIBBY (*To him*)   It's been years since she saw him.

DEBBIE   You already said that, Mama.

LIBBY   Do you think she ever gives him a thought? . . . A forgotten incident.

DEBBIE   Mama, will you please shut up!
(*She runs out the door, leaving it open*)

LIBBY (*Smiling, smoothing it over*)   She's just a little upset—

ROBERT   Don't worry, Mrs. Hirsch—

LIBBY   Who's worried?

ROBERT   I'm told these latent hostilities often come out in the early stages of psychoanalysis. Good night, ladies.
(*He goes out the door, closing it behind him.*

LIBBY's *face reflects her shock and bewilderment. The girls, feeling for her, try to cover)*

JESSIE   Is the Elkens girl still running around with Sidney Scheer?

MINNIE   It's platonic.

SOPHIE   Don't be surprised if there'll be a platonic pregnancy soon.
(*They pause, uncomfortable.* LIBBY *controls her emotions)*

LIBBY   Don't try so hard to change the subject, girls. Come. Let's play.
(*She sits and picks up her cards)*

Curtain

The scene: The Hirsch living room. Later that evening.

At rise: LIBBY *is alone on the stage, straightening the room after the card game. She hears something and goes to look off through the sunroom windows. She comes back, straightens the pillows on the sofa, looks back to see that all is in order, then goes upstairs. As she disappears, the door opens and* DEBBIE *enters, followed by* ROBERT.

ROBERT (*Amused*) So that's what's been eating at you all evening! You don't need a psychoanalyst! You need a memory course!

DEBBIE It's much deeper than that!

ROBERT So occasionally you don't remember my name! I refuse to take it seriously!

DEBBIE But it is serious! It has some hidden meaning!

ROBERT Nonsense! We're going to make this work ourselves.

DEBBIE There's only one way that we can. And I've told you over and over again, but you won't listen! Darling, let's just go some place and get married tonight! !

ROBERT Okay!

DEBBIE Ohhh!
(*He holds her close*)

ROBERT Honey, my mother's having a dress made, with sequins yet, and she's so excited she could bust. As for *your* mother, how can we deprive her of her first course of fresh fruit supreme?

DEBBIE   It's all so barbaric!

ROBERT   I'm more conventional than you are, Debbie. And you may as well face it. As my wife, you'll have to be more conventional, too.

DEBBIE   Don't try to turn me into a reactionary!

ROBERT   I am not a reactionary! I am an Eisenhower Republican!

DEBBIE   Well, I am a Stevenson Democrat!

ROBERT   Just don't say that in front of Mr. McNeal.

DEBBIE   I think you really mean that! Sometimes I don't understand you. You show no individuality. You act as though you were just a pawn in an affluent society.

ROBERT   Come on, Debbie! What's the matter with an affluent society? Would you prefer to live in a nonaffluent society? Well, baby, I'm an expert because *I* have. Boy, was my society nonaffluent—like no money to pay the rent! And I had only one desire—a big, fat, personal, affluent society! I like having money and the clear, economic right to have you as my wife.

DEBBIE   Economic right! What has love got to do with economics? You just are not free!

ROBERT   Free? You mean free like Peter Nemo?

DEBBIE   Yes! Free like Peter Nemo! He lets life wash over him in great waves!

ROBERT   Now what does that mean?

DEBBIE   It means that I am finding out that I still have residual feelings for Peter.

DEAR ME, THE SKY IS FALLING

ROBERT Residual feelings for *Peter? How* residual?

DEBBIE Can't we discuss reality without your becoming angry?

ROBERT Of course I'm angry! What else do you expect me to be?

DEBBIE Is it so odd? Don't you still have feelings for that woman?

ROBERT Don't call her "that woman." Her name is Betty Scott, and, as I have told you over and over again, I once cared for her a great deal.

DEBBIE You do still!

ROBERT I don't still!

DEBBIE You still see her!

ROBERT She is a client of the office. I have to see her on business occasionally. Now, can we forget all about Betty Scott and Peter Nemo?

DEBBIE It is vital to talk things out!

ROBERT And every time we do, we end up beating each other over the head! Oh, I know we get rid of our aggressions that way! Well, I've got a better way to get rid of them. (*He kisses her deeply. Then, suddenly*) What's my name?

DEBBIE What's your name?

ROBERT Yes! What's my name? Quick!

DEBBIE Sonny! Oh—
    (*She runs through the dining room. A door slams offstage*)

ROBERT (*Following*) Debbie! Come back here! . . . Debbie!

LIBBY (*Coming downstairs, carrying her needlepoint*) Robert, what happened?

ROBERT   I don't know, Mrs. Hirsch. I don't know what's happening to her lately.

LIBBY   Well, whatever you said to her and she said to you, you didn't mean it and she didn't mean it.

ROBERT   I'm not so sure.

LIBBY   But I'm sure. And when you're married as long as I am you'll understand women.

ROBERT   I think the best thing to do is to have it out right now—tonight.

LIBBY   Not tonight. When you're emotional is no time to talk—so go home now. (*She moves with him to the door*) Drive carefully and, before you go to bed, take a little Ovaltine—maybe a glass of warm milk and some crackers. Everything will be all right, you'll see.

ROBERT   I want it to be, Mrs. Hirsch. But she has to want it, too.

LIBBY   She does and you do. Good night, darling.

ROBERT   Good night, Mrs. Hirsch.
     (*He goes. She closes the door*)

LIBBY (*Calling*) Debbie . . . Debbie . . .

DEBBIE (*Entering from the dining room*) Mama—I'm sorry about tonight.

LIBBY   It's all right. . . . So what was the big quarrel?

DEBBIE   I don't think it would make any sense to you.

LIBBY   Maybe not but, since you were a little girl, you always told me everything.

33

DEBBIE   Well, Mama, when we first met, he didn't talk very much—but whatever he said was lyric and implausible and terribly exciting. Now he sounds like an I.B.M. machine.

LIBBY   Two people have to make plans.

DEBBIE   I think he has. He sees me in the role of a wife.

LIBBY   What else? Congratulations.

DEBBIE   But *she* is still there, vestigially.

LIBBY   Who is still there vestigially?

DEBBIE   A girl he knew before me.

LIBBY   You mean that woman?

DEBBIE   Her name is Betty Scott.

LIBBY   So what's with him and Betty Scott?

DEBBIE   I don't know.

LIBBY   Well, if you don't know, I think you should find out. If it's still serious, then I'll be the first one to tell you it's a terrible mistake.

DEBBIE   Mama, it is serious—in terms of his psychic mechanism.

LIBBY   Oh, *that.* I was beginning to worry.

DEBBIE   Mama, I may have to worry you, even though I don't want to. He's too dominant for me.

LIBBY   He's a man.

DEBBIE   He wants everything his way.

LIBBY   And you want everything your way.

DEBBIE   We're in massive disagreement—socially, artistically, politically.

DEAR ME, THE SKY IS FALLING

LIBBY Debbie—I know you not from today. I know how you can get panicky over little things. It's like that story I used to read you when you were a little girl: "Chicken Licken."

DEBBIE What light can Chicken Licken throw on the present situation?

LIBBY It wasn't light, it was an acorn. An acorn fell on her head and "Dear me," thought Chicken Licken, "The sky is falling! I have to go run and tell the king!" But first she told it to Henny Penny—and then she told it to Goosey Loosey—and then she told it to Cocky Lockey—and they all got panicky, too. And you know what happened? They all got so frightened they were gobbled up by a treacherous fox.

DEBBIE That's it, Mama! I don't want to be gobbled up. And the only way to make sure of that is to know. People should wait to marry until they really *know* what they're getting.

LIBBY Grandma didn't see Grandpa until the day they were married—and they had nine children and a beautiful golden wedding.

DEBBIE Oh, Mama, you don't understand the deep cleavage between us.

LIBBY Have you changed so much that your mother can't understand? When you were going with Lester Hammil, before you told me, I told *you*. He wasn't for you. I said it first, no? And Howard? And Maxwell? And Sidney? All nice boys, but I understood why.

DEBBIE Why?

LIBBY Why? You gave me the little reasons. You didn't like their jokes; you didn't like their clothes; one wasn't

35

intellectual enough—and Sidney had big ears! But I understood why. And why did I understand why? Because you're like me and I'm like you. And they were the ones you couldn't love or I couldn't love. Right?

DEBBIE   You couldn't love Peter Nemo.

LIBBY   With that beard? And no personal hygiene?

DEBBIE   I was crazy about him—just nuts for him.

LIBBY   So why aren't we embroidering everything with an N?

DEBBIE   He was free—I was inhibited.

LIBBY   You're a lady and he's a bum.

DEBBIE   Mama, will you please stop that!

LIBBY   How can I stop? You're wearing Robert's ring on your finger for eight months. You let Papa make you a big engagement party. You picked out your wedding dress from Bergdorf Goodman. Upstairs is a trousseau fit for a queen. . . . Take my word for it—you're in love. The way you look at each other, I *know* you're in love.

DEBBIE   Mama, I am not you.

LIBBY   So introduce me. Who are you?

DEBBIE   That's what I am trying to work through.

LIBBY   Work through? With an *analyst* you're working through?

DEBBIE   How did you find out?

LIBBY   Tongues slip. Everybody knew it but me. . . . Are you hostile to me?

DEBBIE   Oh, no, Mama! Not knowingly—not willingly! These are involuntary feelings, on a subconscious level.

When I'm me, Mama, I love you. How could you think I didn't?

LIBBY   I love you on all levels. I don't worry about you by the hour; I worry about you on a yearly basis.

DEBBIE   I don't want to be worried about. I just want to be accepted for what I am! And I cannot fight for every breath!
        (PAUL *comes from the pantry carrying his putter and ball bag*)

PAUL   Debbie? What are you doing home so early? Didn't you like the Swedish picture?

DEBBIE   We didn't see it.

LIBBY   They had a quarrel. All of a sudden he's an I.B.M. machine.

DEBBIE   I want to postpone the wedding.
        (PAUL *looks at* LIBBY)

LIBBY (*Significantly*)   Chicken Licken—

DEBBIE   Help me, Papa.

PAUL   This is a very real problem for her, Libby.

LIBBY   And who made it real? That crazy-doctor!

DEBBIE   Mama, please stop clutching at me and accept what I have to do!

PAUL   Debbie, you're a grown-up girl.

LIBBY   Even a grown-up girl has to have a little time to make a decision. . . . So go upstairs, darling, lie down and you'll feel better. (DEBBIE *starts upstairs.* PAUL *goes to the sunroom to put the putter and ball bag away*) I'll bring you a little Ovaltine. . . . Maybe a little warm milk? . . . You want crackers, I'll bring you crackers.

(*After* DEBBIE *is out of sight*) Paul, you knew about the analyst, huh?

PAUL Yes.

LIBBY And Mildred, too?

PAUL And Mildred, too.

LIBBY You just didn't want to worry me?

PAUL That's right.

LIBBY Thank you. So what's his first name?

PAUL What's whose first name?

LIBBY You know who. The man who says he's a dentist —Dr. Evans.

PAUL *We* said he was a dentist. He didn't.

LIBBY (*Opening the telephone book*) So how do I look him up in the book?

PAUL I wouldn't tell you.

LIBBY Paul, I'm just not going to sit here and let—

PAUL There are certain things, they say, that are buried deep down in our subconscious that they have to dig out. People want to be sure they'll be happy before they get married.

LIBBY (*Looking in the telephone book*) Nowadays you have to pay somebody to tell you whether you're happy or not! Everybody wants to be happy twenty-four hours a day. I was happy when the rent was paid, when the children were well, when they brought home A-A-A on their report cards. I was happy. Now people have to turn themselves inside out to know if they're happy or not.

Howard Da Silva, Tresa Hughes, and Gertrude Berg, as
PAUL HIRSCH, MILDRED, and LIBBY HIRSCH.

Michael Baseleon and Jill Kraft, as ROBERT WOLFE and
DEBBIE HIRSCH.

PAUL   Whether you're happy or not, she's going to go on seeing that doctor.

LIBBY   And so will I.

PAUL   Libby, I forbid you to get in contact with him!

LIBBY   Paul, don't forbid me because, if you do, I won't go. And I *have* to go!

PAUL (*Giving up*)   His name is Robert Evans and he's on Sixty-seventh Street—but he wouldn't see you.

LIBBY   So what harm would it be if I call him and ask him to see me if he wouldn't see me?

PAUL   What would you say to him?

LIBBY   What I have to. (*She goes to the phone*)   And he'll listen, because in me he'll see a person who is not repressed by anxiety, who is not frustrated, and who also is *not* a sibling!
   (*She begins dialing the number*)

PAUL (*Ruefully*)   I wish him luck.
   (*She continues dialing*)

Curtain

The scene: DR. EVANS' *office. An afternoon two days later.*

At rise: DR. EVANS *is seated at his desk speaking into the telephone.*

DOCTOR No, your mother hasn't arrived yet, Miss Hirsch. I expect her at any moment. . . . Have you changed your mind about my seeing her? . . . As I told you, Miss Hirsch, the decision must be yours. . . . Yes, in some cases, these interviews with members of the family can be extremely helpful. . . . Well, suppose you arrange to see me here tomorrow morning at nine o'clock. . . . Now, don't worry, Miss Hirsch. . . . Goodbye. (*He hangs up, makes a note. The buzzer sounds. He pushes a button on the phone and picks it up*) Yes? . . . I see. Well, show Mrs. Hirsch in here and I'll come out there to take that call. (*He rises, goes out the door and leaves it open. Then, offstage*) Go right in, Mrs. Hirsch— (LIBBY *enters*) I'll be with you in a moment.

    (LIBBY *observes the room suspiciously. She examines the doctor's degrees, framed on the wall, sees the couch, looks away, looks back. Then she goes over, sits on it a moment, then rises with a disdainful gesture of dismissal. The* DOCTOR *enters*)

LIBBY Thank you, Doctor, for setting aside a little time for me.

40

DOCTOR   I've been looking forward to it for some weeks.

LIBBY   How could you look forward to it? I only know you exist for two days.

DOCTOR (*Closing door*)   I knew you'd find out eventually and ask for an appointment.

LIBBY   How did you know?

DOCTOR   I've heard a great deal about you.

LIBBY   From Debbie?

DOCTOR   Yes.

LIBBY   And Mildred? (*He smiles but no answer*)   I don't see much improvement in my sister's situation with her husband—unless, of course, she's not keeping me posted.

DOCTOR   My relations with my patients are confidential.

LIBBY   My relations are your patients. (*Looking at the couch*)   No matter what you say to the contrary, Doctor, I will not lie on that couch.

DOCTOR   Why should you? I think you'll find that chair very comfortable. It swivels.

LIBBY (*Sitting in the chair*)   Thank you. When I talk to people I like to look at their faces. You don't?

DOCTOR (*Sitting in his chair*)   Sometimes people don't like to look at *my* face.

LIBBY   I don't mind. . . . It's not what people say—it's what they look like when they're saying it.

DOCTOR   I agree. There *is* an advanced school that's abandoning the couch for those very reasons.

LIBBY   Five minutes and I'm already advanced.

DOCTOR   Well, here you are, Mrs. Hirsch. No mystery about an analyst's office. . . . Usually, the patient lies on the couch and I sit behind him, and we talk, and I take notes. From time to time, in special cases, I use certain visual aids to help. Like those Rorschach tests. (*Lifting a card from his desk*)   They're ink blots and I sometimes ask patients what these blots remind them of. The mental images they conjure up help to indicate what they're really thinking of.

LIBBY   To me, it conjures up a bunch of soup greens. . . . And, Doctor, you're cooking up some soup.

DOCTOR   Now what soup precisely shall *we* talk about?

LIBBY   My daughter.

DOCTOR   What is it you wish to know?

LIBBY   I wish to know what will come out of these ink blots. That is what I wish to know. And I also wish to know what you're telling her and what she's telling you. Does she say that I'm a clutcher?

DOCTOR   Do you think you're a clutcher?

LIBBY   I try to do what's right.

DOCTOR   What do you think is right, Mrs. Hirsch?

LIBBY   What I think is right? What the whole world thinks is right. Right is right. And wrong is wrong.

DOCTOR   Surely you'll agree, Mrs. Hirsch, that some people are troubled by what is right and what is wrong—and require help.

LIBBY   Sick people. My Debbie is not sick so don't make her sick.

DOCTOR Are you saying that you reject all psychotherapy out of hand?

LIBBY No. I don't live in a cocoon. I try to keep up with the things that are going on in the world—including even psychiatry.

DOCTOR Are you succeeding?

LIBBY Are you? . . . Has it made you a happy man?

DOCTOR Fairly.

LIBBY To me, fairly wouldn't be enough to help other people to be happy.

DOCTOR Yes, but I'm trained. I'm objective.

LIBBY Are you married?

DOCTOR Yes.

LIBBY You have children?

DOCTOR No.

LIBBY I have four. But you still have time. You're so *young*, aren't you, Doctor?

DOCTOR Are you saying that you have less confidence in me because you think I'm immature?

LIBBY *You* said immature—I said young. . . . How old are you, Doctor?

DOCTOR How old are you, Mrs. Hirsch?

LIBBY Over twenty-one.

DOCTOR Over twenty-one.

LIBBY But you haven't been practicing very long?

DOCTOR Fourteen years, Mrs. Hirsch.

LIBBY   But that includes interning?

DOCTOR   No, Mrs. Hirsch, that does not include interning.

LIBBY   Oh.

DOCTOR   Now, shall we come to the point of your visit?

LIBBY   Doctor, as Debbie's mother, I think it's best for her to marry Robert Wolfe. They love each other and nobody has a right to interfere.

DOCTOR   Your daughter came to me of her own free will, Mrs. Hirsch. Now hasn't it been obvious to you that she's been troubled?

LIBBY   Doctor, all young girls, just before they get married, begin to have doubts. I loved my Paul very much and I had doubts. But we got married and, by the time my first child came along, all the doubts went out with the ashes. So it will be with Debbie! (*Rising*)   So you won't be seeing her any more. (*Goes to the door*)   If there's any fee . . .

DOCTOR (*Rises*)   Do you still have ashes in your home, Mrs. Hirsch?

LIBBY   Ashes? Years ago we converted to an oil burner.

DOCTOR   And thus you found a more efficient way to heat your house? By the same token, there's a more efficient way to deal with Debbie's doubts as well. And I think I can help her, Mrs. Hirsch. So please, sit down.

LIBBY (*After a pause she returns to the chair and sits*) How long will it take?

DOCTOR (*Sitting*)   I don't know.

LIBBY   One week? Two weeks?

DOCTOR   My guess would be rather more than that.

LIBBY But the invitations are all ready to be mailed out.

DOCTOR Aren't invitations occasionally withheld?

LIBBY Oh. I see. So that's what you'd like. Let me tell you something, Doctor. My family's problems will not be solved in a psychiatrist's office. Family problems should be solved in the family. What else is a family for?

DOCTOR A family or a mother?

LIBBY Yes, Doctor, a mother! And as Debbie's mother, I can save you a little time. My Debbie was a seven-months baby. She came early, but she developed late. She walked late—she talked late—and she didn't wear a foundation garment till she was fifteen and a half. (*Opening her purse and taking out a small leather folder*) Here—here's my Debbie at fifteen and a half— a baby! (*He takes the folder*) So romance came late, too. Then along came a fellow named Peter Nemo and believe me, Paul and I had plenty of sleepless nights.

DOCTOR Why?

LIBBY Why? Because we knew him, that's why. He came from a very nice family. . . . They gave him every advantage but, all of a sudden, he became a Jimmy Dean. And—after all these years—Debbie had to go and meet him again. Suffice it to say, pop went the weasel.

DOCTOR How—pop went the weasel?

LIBBY (*Giving him a look, rejecting his obvious meaning*) Not my daughter. We know how we brought her up.

DOCTOR Why do you think she was attracted to Peter Nemo?

LIBBY Why? Because he was attracted to her. He flattered

her—he complimented her. He told her she was a literary genius which—even as a mother—I tell you she is not. . . . If she could see him again and compare him to her Robert, she'd see what she's got.

DOCTOR   And you think that would solve everything?

LIBBY   No. I admit there are other problems. She worries because he once knew someone else— (*He hands her the picture and she returns it to her purse*)   and my sister is adding fuel to the fire, too. And her father's not much help either. I don't understand that man lately. All he's thinking about is retiring to Florida. . . . I suppose it's not easy for a father to lose his last daughter.

DOCTOR   Is it easy for a mother?

LIBBY   Doctor, I want my Debbie married. And you know why? Because I want her to have a full life as a woman and as a person—and I say every woman should have a decent man of her own. And I don't care what Freud says.

DOCTOR   That's exactly what Freud says, Mrs. Hirsch.

LIBBY   So why are you advising against it?

DOCTOR   Debbie and I are trying to find out what she needs to make her ready for marriage—ready to leave home and commit herself permanently to another human being.

LIBBY   (*Rising and going to the door*)   Well, Doctor, in five years from now, when you find out my Debbie's ready, she will already have weaned two children.

DOCTOR   (*Has risen with her*)   Mrs. Hirsch, don't declare war on me.

46

DEAR ME, THE SKY IS FALLING

LIBBY (*Opening the door*) Doctor, you said it—I didn't. Is there a fee?

DOCTOR There's no fee, Mrs. Hirsch.

LIBBY Thank you. And, oh, Doctor, you are cordially invited to attend the wedding of Debbie Hirsch to Mr. Robert Wolfe on June eighteenth at the Hampshire House—you won't even have to R.S.V.P.

> (*She exits. He closes the door, pats his face with his handkerchief, takes the dictaphone microphone from a drawer of the desk, then sits and begins to dictate*)

DOCTOR Met today with mother of Patient Four-seven-four. The interview sheds a new light on the patient's basic conflict. It is obvious that she was over-loved, over-protected and, I suspect, over-indulged. The mother, on the other hand, is classically possessive, extraordinarily imposing and—well—she's a lulu.

Curtain

Act Two

ACT TWO

The scene: The Hirsch living room. Sunday morning.

At rise: PAUL *is practicing his putting on the carpet.* DEB-
BIE *comes in the front door.*

DEBBIE   Hi ya, Pop!

PAUL   Debbie! Where did you go so early this morning? I
thought you liked to sleep late on Sunday? (*He puts the
golf balls in his jacket pocket*)   What happened? Where
was the fire?

DEBBIE   I had an extra-special session with Dr. Evans.

PAUL   Oh?

DEBBIE   Papa, did you know Mama went to see him yes-
terday?

PAUL   Did you ever try to stop your mother?

DEBBIE   Yes. But not this time. I knew she was going. The
doctor asked my permission and I thought, why not?

PAUL   So what did the doctor suggest?

DEBBIE   Everything is falling into place. I am beginning
to see the situation clearly.

PAUL   I would also like to see it clearly.

DEBBIE   Well—the warp and the woof of it is that I didn't
agree to marry out of my own free will. I did it to please

51

Mama. I'm fantasied as something I'm not—well-rounded, sophisticated, beautiful, responsive to his career—The dichotomy of my super—

PAUL   Debbie, don't use such words with me. Talk like my own Debbie.

DEBBIE   I hope this doesn't hurt you, Papa, but I have to break it off.

PAUL   Break it off? Why? What happened?

DEBBIE   Papa, he and I just don't agree about anything.

PAUL   What can I do?

DEBBIE   Be on my side, Papa, because—I have to move out of here.

PAUL   Move out? Why should you move out right now, at a time when you need your mother and me the most?

DEBBIE   I mustn't lean any more. I have to be strong.

PAUL   Where will you go?

DEBBIE   I'll go and live with Aunt Mildred.

PAUL   Three blocks away? I'm sorry, but that's strong?

DEBBIE   It's a first step. And then I'll look for an apartment in New York. Then, maybe I can sit down at a typewriter and create. That way, I'll be surrounded by reality instead of illusion.

PAUL   Sometimes it's not easy to tell one from the other.

DEBBIE   (A pause) Is your putting getting any better, Papa?

PAUL   I'm still having trouble with my left wrist.

DEBBIE   What you need is a lot of practice. You'll get that in Florida.

PAUL   You think your mama will go to Florida with you living with your Aunt Mildred?

DEBBIE   You've got to make her.

PAUL   And if she doesn't want to go—I'm supposed to go alone?

DEBBIE   Papa—you and Mama are—all right together?

PAUL   What a question. (*She starts up the stairs*)   No—no—don't go! What are you talking about?

DEBBIE   Nothing. . . . Nothing.

PAUL   Something! Something! You heard something maybe?

DEBBIE   No.

PAUL   Don't insinuate. . . . Rumors you heard? (*She shrugs*)   Rumors about a woman? (*She shrugs*)   About Selma Harris?

DEBBIE   Yes.

PAUL   Debbie, last year we had a Christmas party down at the place and I had a few drinks and I snapped Selma Harris's garter. So she cornered me and chased me around the office a couple of times and that's the whole thing with Selma Harris.

DEBBIE   Papa, talk to me as an equal!

PAUL   All right. For fifteen years, Selma Harris worked for me. She was a very capable, intelligent woman. What I didn't realize was, in the back of her head, she had romantic ideas about me—and she talked too much about them. So, it was best for her to resign.

DEBBIE   Then there's no more to it than that, Papa?

PAUL   What kind of a question is that for a daughter to
ask a father? . . . But I'll answer it. No. And you know
why? (*She shakes her head*)   Because the way to solve
problems is not to have any. For a man to risk his whole
set-up in life for one hour of pleasure, he'd have to be
crazy. And it isn't always easy, Debbie, because sometimes a man's eyes rove— And what kind of a way is that
for a father to talk to a daughter?

DEBBIE   A very nice way!
       (*He touches her cheek.* LIBBY *enters from the out-
       side door, carrying her purse and a shopping bag of
       groceries.*)

LIBBY (*Gaily, as she puts the bag of groceries on the
telephone bench*)   What a beautiful summer's day!
You know what I just saw? Buds on the lilac bushes!
And you know what that means? It means summer is
just around the corner so we'll give the season a little
push! And tonight we'll have a little cook-out outside. I
already have steaks marinating in soy sauce, and we'll
have a salad with canned asparagus, because Robert
loves them—

DEBBIE   Robert is *not* coming!

LIBBY   We'll see. (*Looking at the grocery list*)   He only
gave me two cans of asparagus and I ordered three.
Well— Paul, darling, take the cobwebs off the barbecue
—get out the cushions for the porch furniture—and we'll
have a regular old-fashioned Sunday-night supper tonight. Who knows who'll drop in?

DEBBIE   Mama, don't be casual. I know what you did.

PAUL (*Hastily, going to the pantry door*)   I'll clean the
barbecue, then I'll run out to Pine Tree for nine holes—

LIBBY Only one highball, and no peanuts. Don't forget your diverticulitis.

DEBBIE Papa, please stay!

PAUL No, sweetheart. This is time for girl talk.
(*He goes*)

LIBBY (*Trying to avoid the issue with* DEBBIE—*laughs*) Girl talk! You know, Debbie, that I secretly tried to lea:n to play golf so I wouldn't be a grass widow on Sundays. But, you know, my swing—my swing has no follow-through. (*She swings an imaginary club*) Look at that! Nothing!

DEBBIE Mama, you did me a favor. Your session with Dr. Evans solidified my determination. I am moving out.

LIBBY Where are you moving? Aunt Mildred's?

DEBBIE Only for a while.

LIBBY That means I can cancel the Hampshire House?

DEBBIE I'm afraid so.

LIBBY There's no Supreme Court I can go to?

DEBBIE No.

LIBBY Does Robert know?

DEBBIE I haven't spoken to Robert for two days, so I'm sure he suspects. I think he'll be delighted it's over. . . . I'd better go and sort out what I'm going to take!
(DEBBIE *runs up the stairs.* LIBBY *looks after her, then sits on the telephone bench, picks up the phone and dials a number*)

LIBBY Hello! . . . Yes. . . . Fine. . . . How's Robert enjoying his brunch? . . . Good! . . . Debbie is fine—a little emotional, but who takes that seriously? Listen, darling, I want you and Robert to come over tonight. We're having a little cook-out outside. . . . You can talk freely. What is it? . . . He saw who last night? . . . You mean that woman? How do you know? . . . (DEBBIE *starts down the stairs, carrying one stocking. She stops and listens*) Well, it could be anybody's compact on the front seat! . . . So what were the initials? . . . B.S.? . . . Don't jump to conclusions! . . . You're telling me that Robert is a fine boy? (*She sees* DEBBIE) Don't hang— (*Hand over the mouthpiece, to* DEBBIE) You're looking for your stockings, darling? They're upstairs in the left-hand—

DEBBIE   He saw her last night!

LIBBY   I don't know who saw who last night.

DEBBIE   I'm not surprised! I think we can safely say *that is that!*
            (*She runs upstairs*)

LIBBY (*Calling after her*) That is not that! Robert's not that kind of a boy! Do you think he'd go off with somebody else just because you had a quarrel? And if that is that, it's your fault! (*Into the phone*) I'm back. Now we have a real problem. . . . If you knew she was such a designing woman, why didn't you put your foot down before this? . . . I should call her? If anybody should call her, you should call her. . . . Well, if she knows your voice, disguise your voice. . . . I don't care if it's Butterfield 8 or Buttercup 8! Don't give me the number because I'm not even listening! . . . (*She picks up a pencil, moistens the tip in her mouth and writes*) Well, I'm thinking. . . . I'll see you tonight at the barbecue. Goodbye, Hortense. (*She hangs up, hesitates, and then dials, consulting the number she jotted down*)

DEAR ME, THE SKY IS FALLING

Hello? Is this Mrs. Scott? . . . I am calling to invite you and your husband to the wedding of Deborah Hirsch to Robert Wolfe on June eighteenth. . . . I'm only calling because I know you're friends . . .

MILDRED (*Rushing in the outside door*) Libby?!

LIBBY Oh, well . . . I'm sorry you won't be in town. Goodbye. (*She hangs up and goes to the table near the stairs, where she industriously addresses wedding-invitation envelopes*) You came before breakfast, Mildred?

MILDRED Libby, I barged in because I have to ask you one question! Just one question, that's all!

LIBBY So what's your one question?

PAUL (*Sticking his head in through the pantry door*) Libby, you got any sandpaper in the kitchen?

LIBBY No, Paul, but there's sandpaper in the garage.

PAUL (*To* MILDRED) I'm cleaning the barbecue. Libby is marinating steaks.

MILDRED She's also addressing envelopes. Why do you need invitations, Libby? The wedding's off.

LIBBY Who told you?

MILDRED I heard it from the horse's mouth.

LIBBY So what do you want to ask me with your one question?

MILDRED Why did my David communicate with me this morning?
    (PAUL *has come in to listen*)

LIBBY I didn't even know he communicated.

MILDRED   After two years! Like a bolt from the blue, he calls me up!

LIBBY   You should be glad the line wasn't busy.

MILDRED   That's all you have to say, Libby? I know you—not from today. I've been your sister a long time.

LIBBY   Yeah, and I've been your sister a long time.

MILDRED   Did you have anything to do with it?

LIBBY   So what did he want?

MILDRED   To chat!

LIBBY   Did he ask for Paul? Did he ask for me?

MILDRED   He asked! Also for Debbie! He also asked—can you imagine?—if I could have dinner with him tonight!

LIBBY   So was it yes, or was it no?

MILDRED   I tried no but it came out yes.

LIBBY   So bring him to the barbecue tonight!

MILDRED   No. He's coming to pick me up and we're going to drive up to Connecticut someplace—like old times! And it has to happen on a Sunday. My hair is like an O-Cedar mop. My beauty parlor isn't open. I tried to get Mr. Maurice at home, but he's unlisted. Do you think Debbie would set my hair for me?

LIBBY   Go up and ask her—and tell her I bought some hair spray if she wants to use it.

MILDRED   (*Going upstairs*) Do you think I should wear bangs again, Libby?

LIBBY   If bangs will make you happy, wear bangs. (MILDRED *disappears.* LIBBY *sees* PAUL) Wasn't it amazing that David should just call her up today?

PAUL (*Staring at her stonily*) No, I don't think it's very amazing, Libby.

LIBBY So I gave it a little push. It was time.

PAUL Time for what? Time there shouldn't be a spare room in Mildred's apartment?

LIBBY It's the psychological time for Mildred to solve her problems.

PAUL Libby, what else is it the psychological time for? Who else have you called up? What other plans have you set in motion?

LIBBY Paul, let me tell you something. On June eighteenth, your daughter, Debbie, is marrying Robert Wolfe. (*The doorbell rings*) I'll go. I'm expecting somebody.

PAUL It may also be somebody *I'm* expecting.
(*He goes to the door*)

LIBBY Oh, you made plans, too? We'll have a lot of company.
(PAUL *opens the door and* MR. *and* MRS. SCHLINGER *enter. They are in their middle years*)

PAUL Hello, Mr. Schlinger.

MR. SCHLINGER How do you do?

PAUL Mrs. Schlinger?

MRS. SCHLINGER How do you do, Mr. Hirsch.

PAUL (*To* LIBBY) Darling, this is Mr. and Mrs. Schlinger. (*To them*) This is my wife, Mrs. Hirsch.

MRS. SCHLINGER How do you do, Mrs. Hirsch?
(*They shake hands*)

LIBBY How do you do?

MR. SCHLINGER   How do you do?

PAUL (*Closing the door*)   Darling, I bumped into Mr. Schlinger last week. Mr. and Mrs. Schlinger want to look at the house—

MRS. SCHLINGER   With a view to purchase—

PAUL   Mrs. Schlinger would like to move out into the suburbs.

LIBBY (*To* PAUL—*meaningfully*)   I wish you had prepared me for this unilateral decision. (*To the* SCHLINGERS) We're so preoccupied with our daughter's forthcoming marriage—

MRS. SCHLINGER   Oh, don't apologize! We won't be long! We know the general layout of these houses. My aunt is Mrs. Solowey. She lived on this block. Hers was a house exactly like yours. They moved to Florida.

LIBBY   Because she has asthma.

MRS. SCHLINGER   You'll be neighbors again in Florida, Mr. Hirsch tells me.

LIBBY   Well, we'll see. . . . Aren't you interested in a young house? A ranch-type?

MRS. SCHLINGER   We're looking for a good buy!

MR. SCHLINGER   We're prepared to pay cash.

PAUL   Shall we start with the upstairs?

LIBBY   Debbie is upstairs doing Mildred's hair.

PAUL   I'll show you the master bedroom—

LIBBY   Show the bathroom, dear—

PAUL   Sweetheart, do you want to show the house or shall I?

LIBBY No, darling, you show it. (*To them*) It's an old-fashioned bathroom. We never got around to fixing the plumbing.

MRS. SCHLINGER If it's a bargain—

PAUL It's a nice-sized bathroom. And there's another bathroom connecting two bedrooms—

LIBBY No tub.

PAUL It has a shower!

LIBBY It needs retiling.

PAUL We have an estimate from a man—very inexpensive!

LIBBY We have another estimate for the pipes—not so inexpensive.

MRS. SCHLINGER What's the matter with the pipes?

PAUL (*To* LIBBY) They're copper!

LIBBY (*To* MRS. SCHLINGER) They're small and it takes the hot water a long time to go upstairs.

MRS. SCHLINGER If the price is right—

PAUL (*Taking* MRS. SCHLINGER's *hand and helping her up the stairs before him*) We have storm windows on all the windows!
(MR. SCHLINGER *follows*)

MRS. SCHLINGER Oh, that's good!
(MILDRED *starts downstairs*)

PAUL This is my sister-in-law.

MILDRED How do you do?

PAUL They're looking at the house with a view to purchase.

MILDRED (*Coming on down*) I hope you like it. (PAUL *and the* SCHLINGERS *go upstairs*) Libby, you better go upstairs and talk to Debbie. She's in a black mood!

LIBBY Out of a clear sky on a Sunday he brings people to look at the house.

MILDRED Libby, will you do me a favor and talk to Deborah? Because I told her it wouldn't be convenient for her to move into my apartment tonight—on account of David—you should have heard the outburst.

LIBBY I can imagine.

MILDRED What am I going to do about my hair?

LIBBY (*Moving to the pantry door*) Come. I'll do it for you.
    (*The doorbell rings*)

MILDRED Whoever it is, Libby, please make it short! I want to get home in time to change and put on a face!
    (MILDRED *goes through the pantry door.* LIBBY *looks at the front door, then back to be sure* MILDRED *is gone. Then she goes to the front door, opens it and admits* PETER NEMO. *He's a graduate of the Beat Generation, young and curiously handsome*)

LIBBY (*Cordially*) Hello, Peter. Come in. . . . I see you shaved off your beard. I'm very glad you got the message I left for you at the Unicorn Coffee House.

PETER Loud and clear. Where is it?

LIBBY (*Indicating the A&P box on a chair just inside the sunroom*) Right here. I didn't want it to get broken. That's why I asked you to come and pick it up yourself.

PETER I know you well, Mrs. Hirsch. The last thing you want is for me to come here, so why do you want me to come here?

LIBBY   To pick up your present.

PETER   Can I see her?

LIBBY   Why not?

PETER   You *want* me to see her. Why?

LIBBY   What kind of a question is that, Peter?

PETER   Because I think you're still trying to run the world. . . . Why am I surprised? The world is run by women.

LIBBY   Don't you like women?

PETER   Women. Not mothers.

LIBBY   You have a very nice mother. You don't love your mother?

PETER   I love her. She lives in Philadelphia and, as long as she stays there, I love her.

LIBBY   Maybe you'd like to shoot your father?

PETER   I don't have to. My mother took care of him a long time ago.

LIBBY (*Calling up the stairs*)   Debbie! There's somebody down here to see you, dear.

DEBBIE'S VOICE   Who is it?

LIBBY   Come down. (*Turning to* PETER)   Nice seeing you, Peter. Excuse me.
         (*She goes through the pantry door.* DEBBIE *comes running downstairs and stops abruptly on the landing as she sees* PETER)

PETER (*Looking at her appraisingly*)   Like it's been a couple of light years.

DEBBIE   Peter—what are you doing here?

63

DEAR ME, THE SKY IS FALLING

PETER   Congratulations. I saw a picture of you and your lawyer in the paper. He is a high-class demigod.

DEBBIE (*Coming down one step*)   Yes.

PETER   Like I say, it's been a couple of light years.

DEBBIE (*Nervously, coming to the bottom of the stairs*) Whose fault is that?

PETER   Mine. Yours. Your mother's. Your addiction to the middle middle class. Your yearning to be free—and your fear of being free. Your fear of your yearning and your yearning to fear.

DEBBIE   Is that a new poem you wrote?

PETER   I think it's a new poem I'm going to write. How's your novel?

DEBBIE   Unfinished and unsung.

PETER   Pity. . . . It had pith.

DEBBIE   Why did you come here?

PETER   Your mother left a message at the coffee house for me to come and pick up my present—my mobile—intended to swing free in your interior-decorated cell.

DEBBIE   My mother had no right to do that!

PETER   I thank her and so should you.

DEBBIE   The last thing I'll ever do is thank her for this.

PETER   You still shine.

DEBBIE   Will you go away, Peter?

PETER   Hmm-umm. You shine. You sing. You radiate. I want you.

64

DEBBIE   I fell for that line once, Peter. I'm not going to fall for it again. I'm in analysis now. I'm getting stronger.

PETER   Do I figure on the couch?

DEBBIE   Yes.

PETER   Did you tell the doctor that you walked into the light for a moment—then stepped back into the dark?

DEBBIE   Will you stop talking like that!

PETER   That's the way your mother wants me to talk.

DEBBIE   How do you know the way my mother wants you to talk?

PETER   Because I'm a mother-hag-ridden expert. You are to face me, Debbie. You are to see that I am real. That's what she wants.

DEBBIE   That is exactly what she *doesn't* want!

PETER   That's the mother brain revolving in space. Honey, I'm your unfinished business. I stand between you and your bureaucrat. You are to see that I am unkempt and woolly—incapable of self-support. You're to want him more because you want me less. You're not to remember that there was a winter night and a zebra skin rug. That zebra has become a bone in your throat, Debbie, and your mother wants you to cough. So look at me, and cough me up, Debbie.

DEBBIE   Peter—maybe—when I move out of this house—we could see each other again.

PETER   What time is it now?

DEBBIE   (*Looking at her watch*)   Almost twelve.

PETER   There's a bus for Nyack at twelve-forty. . . . And from Nyack we can hike to my primeval hill and sit in the sun. Come with me, Debbie. I really need you to function, baby. Oh, how I need you to function.

(*He takes her in his arms and kisses her deeply.* PAUL, MRS. SCHLINGER *and* MR. SCHLINGER *start downstairs*)

MRS. SCHLINGER   How much oil do you use?

PAUL   Well, it averages—Debbie! (DEBBIE *and* PETER *step apart*)   It averages for the year about fifteen dollars a month. That's not bad considering it's a big house.

DEBBIE (*Embarrassed*)   Papa, you remember Peter Nemo?

PAUL (*Icily*)   Yes, I remember him. When you went to school with him. Mr. and Mrs. Schlinger, this is my daughter, Debbie, and this is Peter Nemo, the only home-grown poet we ever raised in this neighborhood.

MR. SCHLINGER   How do you do?

MRS. SCHLINGER   I heard you were getting married, Miss Hirsch! (*Moving on to shake* PETER's *hand*)   Congratulations, young man!

PETER (*Entering into the spirit*)   Thank you very much! . . . I'm the wrong young man.

MRS. SCHLINGER   Oh. Pardon me.

PETER   It's quite all right. . . . Debbie, any point in my grounding myself here?

DEBBIE   Yes. Wait.

PAUL   Yes, wait! You, too, Debbie. (*To the* SCHLINGERS) So what do you think about the house?

MRS. SCHLINGER   I'd like to look at the kitchen.

MR. SCHLINGER   Then it boils down to how much you want.

66

PAUL   Make us an offer. We turned down thirty-six thousand last year.

MRS. SCHLINGER   Well, we wouldn't dream of going that far, with all the alterations we'd have to make. Could I see the kitchen?

PAUL (*Going to the pantry door, calling*)   Libby—

LIBBY (*Entering immediately, almost clipping him with the door*)   Oh, you're leaving! I'm sorry you don't like the house. Still here, Peter? (*To* DEBBIE) Wasn't it nice of Peter to drop in personally, Debbie?

PAUL   Libby, they *do* like the house.

MRS. SCHLINGER   Our plan would be—bring the outside inside! Lots of glass!

LIBBY   That's a big investment for such an old house. I don't think it would be worth it.

MRS. SCHLINGER   If you think you could accept thirty-four-five, it's a deal!

LIBBY (*Opening the door*)   We'll think about it and let you know. Goodbye, Mr. Schlinger. Goodbye, Mrs. Schlinger.

MRS. SCHLINGER (*Indicating the pantry door*)   I would still like to see the kitchen.

LIBBY   It's a mess now. Come back some other time.
        (MRS. SCHLINGER *exits.* PAUL *is walking* MR. SCHLINGER *to the door*)

PAUL   Mr. Schlinger, I'll call you at your office tomorrow. We'll talk business. Thank you for coming.
        (MR. SCHLINGER *exits.* LIBBY *closes the door*)

LIBBY Paul, come in the kitchen. I'll fix you a cup of coffee—

DEBBIE (*Sarcastically*) Mama—thanks for calling up Peter!

LIBBY You said to send it back and I didn't want it to get broken.

PAUL I don't like to sound like a father, Debbie, but I'd appreciate it if you and this young man would complete your business as soon as possible!
(*He goes through the pantry door*)

LIBBY Peter, if you want something, just holler. . . . And when you write home, give my love to your mother —and also your poor father.
(*She goes*)

PETER Are you ready to split or not?

DEBBIE If you wait just one minute, we'll be on our way to Nyack!
(*She runs up the stairs. The door bursts open and* ROBERT *rushes in*)

ROBERT Debbie! Where are you? I have to talk to you!

PETER Hi, old daddy!

ROBERT Who are you?

PETER Name is Nemo—

ROBERT *Peter* Nemo—

PETER Age: twenty-six; address: two-o-seven Mulberry Street; occupation: student of the whims of nature, or naturalist, if you prefer. Presently unemployed but comfortably situated by the extreme kindness of the State Unemployment Insurance Act.

ROBERT   I know about you.

PETER   I know about *you*—more than you know.

ROBERT   I'm not interested!

PETER   I am your catalytic agent.

ROBERT   You're my nothing! Debbie!

PETER   I'm taking her away from you! I'll make her into a whole woman with something to say and a way to say it.

ROBERT   It won't take me long to say what *I* have to say, and then you can make her into a whole anything you like! (*He bounds up the stairs, calling*) Debbie! Debbie!

   (*The phone rings.* PAUL *comes from the pantry*)

PAUL (*To* PETER)   You still here? (*Picks up the phone*) Hello. . . . Hello, Charlie. . . . What? . . . No, Charlie, you got it wrong— (LIBBY *opens the pantry door a few inches, then retreats*) I'm not buying out *your* business. You're buying out *my* business. . . . For a hundred and fifty thousand? Who said that? . . . Hold everything, Charlie. I'll see you in the morning! (*He hangs up the phone and shouts*) Libby!

   (LIBBY *comes from the pantry*)

LIBBY   What's the excitement? Where's the fire?

PAUL   Libby, did you call Charlie Finkel and tell him I changed my mind?

LIBBY   I called *Mrs.* Finkel. She's a member of my sisterhood.

PAUL   I don't care if she's a member of your red-riding hood! (MILDRED *comes from the pantry. Her hair is half up in pin curls*) What did you tell her?

LIBBY Well, I just told her we were thinking of retiring to Florida and sit in the sun and enjoy—and she said she and Charlie were thinking the same thing—and I said—

PAUL You said it would be a good idea if the shoe were on the other foot—for a hundred and fifty thousand.

LIBBY It was just two women talking.

PAUL Well, this is a man and a woman talking, Libby! And this cuts it right down the middle!

LIBBY Paul, I didn't mean any harm. And if you think Charlie Finkel's business isn't a bargain at a hundred and fifty. . . . Aaron Bender at the bank would give you the money in a minute.

PAUL Did you call Aaron Bender at the bank?

LIBBY I called Mrs. Bender.

PAUL Oh, Libby, you have gone too far!

DEBBIE'S VOICE (*From upstairs*) I will not tolerate your coming here and accusing me—

ROBERT'S VOICE If it wasn't you, who was it?

DEBBIE'S VOICE It's a matter of complete indifference to me.

 (*They come downstairs.* DEBBIE *has changed clothes*)

ROBERT Well, *somebody* called her up!

DEBBIE I swear I didn't!

ROBERT I have been trying to be patient. I have been ready to go along. I have been eager to give you every possible break until you were settled in your mind, but it's hopeless unless there's mutual trust.

DEBBIE   I tell you I did not call that woman—which is more than I can say for you.

ROBERT   What does that mean?

DEBBIE   You saw her last night.

ROBERT   Yes! I saw her last night! On business!

DEBBIE   There's no need to be so defensive.

ROBERT   I'm not being defensive! Mrs. Scott is my client and I had to see her! And what's more I *wanted* to see her! I've been upset and I was glad to talk to somebody who was pleasant to me!

DEBBIE   How pleasant was she?

ROBERT   Don't try that kind of sarcasm with me, Debbie! You're supposed to trust me, too! You have no right to invade my privacy! Above all, you had no right to call her!

DEBBIE   I didn't call her! I wouldn't be found dead talking to that woman!

PETER   We got a bus to make, Deb.

ROBERT   You shut up!

PAUL   Yeah, you get out of this house!

LIBBY   Robert . . . I called her.

MILDRED   So! It's been some morning with the voice with the smile on the telephone, Libby?

LIBBY   Later, darling?

MILDRED   Sure, darling. I bet you also called David, darling. Everything she takes in her own hands! Well, I've had just about enough.

ROBERT   So have I. My mother warned me against you, Mrs. Hirsch. But I liked you. I felt there was a directness about you, and a brain and a heart. But, Mrs. Hirsch, I'm not a toy and I prefer to manage my own life! I am sorry I misjudged you, Debbie. I will go to any ends to make this work.

DEBBIE   Except you refuse to understand my inner problems—my underlying psychic mechanism!

ROBERT   There you go with that damn psychiatry again!

DEBBIE   You could do with some psychiatry yourself!

ROBERT   You want my considered diagnosis of your problem? You are a split personality. You're split three ways —and get this crystal clear! I've no intention of taking on a girl, an analyst, and a mother!!
    (*He rushes out the door, slamming it behind him*)

DEBBIE   Goodbye, Pa. Goodbye, Ma. Are you ready, Peter?
    (PETER *has opened the door and preceded her out*)

PAUL   Where are you going?

DEBBIE   Somewhere near Nyack!!!
    (*She slams the door behind her*)

LIBBY   Paul, stop her! Mildred, stop her. Somebody, stop her!

PAUL   How? What should I use? A lasso?

LIBBY   Paul, don't stand like a statue! It's the end with Robert! This is not what she wants and I know it!

PAUL   And when I see what your finagling has done to this family, I want what I want and I know it! (*Goes into the sunroom for his golf clubs, his hand in his coat pocket*) What did I do with the car keys?

DEAR ME, THE SKY IS FALLING

LIBBY   In the pantry—

PAUL   You know everything, don't you, Libby?

LIBBY   Where are you going? I've got steaks marinating.

PAUL   I'm going out to the club to see Joe Weldon about one of his houses in Florida—occupancy for one.
(*He goes out through the pantry*)

MILDRED (*Tying a scarf over her pin curls*)   If I were you, Libby, I wouldn't count on its being occupancy for one. I wouldn't be a bit surprised if Miss Selma Harris might like very much to live in Florida. And if you don't believe me, why don't you make *another* call and ask her for yourself?
(*She goes, slamming the front door behind her. After a beat,* LIBBY *rises, goes to the phone, changes her mind, hesitates and then goes with purpose to the phone. She sits, dials, almost hangs up, then continues*)

LIBBY   Hello? Is this Dr. Evans' office? . . . Could you get a message to him, please? . . . Have him call Mrs. Hirsch at Beverly six-o-four-one-four. . . . Please, tell him it's an emergency.

Curtain

The scene: DR. EVANS' *office. Late that afternoon.*

At rise: DR. EVANS *is alone. There is a knock at the door. He opens it, revealing* LIBBY.

DOCTOR Come in, Mrs. Hirsch.

LIBBY Thank you, Doctor, for putting aside a little time for me—especially on a Sunday.

DOCTOR It appeared to be urgent.

LIBBY It is. (*He closes the door*) Doctor, could you take me on as a pupil?

DOCTOR I'm not a teacher.

LIBBY A patient, then. I don't like to say "patient" because when I do I smell ether.

DOCTOR (*Looking her right in the eye*) What makes you think you need therapy?

LIBBY You're staring at me, Doctor. It makes me very uncomfortable.

DOCTOR (*His eye still on her*) As I said before, that's the reason many people prefer the couch.

LIBBY The couch?

DOCTOR The couch. I'd be behind you.

LIBBY As a physician, do you recommend it?

DOCTOR It's entirely up to you.

LIBBY You wouldn't tell anybody?

DOCTOR Do you think I would?

(She shakes her head, takes off her coat and places it on the chair, then, carrying her purse, she lies on the couch)

LIBBY It's very comfortable. Of course, I like a harder mattress. . . . Sometimes I have a little trouble with my sacroiliac. Do you ever have trouble with your back, Doctor?

DOCTOR *(Sitting in his chair behind her)* Did you come to see me about your back?

LIBBY No.

DOCTOR Then why?

LIBBY Because I did something wrong. . . . Many things wrong. Shall I enumerate?

DOCTOR If you like.

LIBBY Doctor, you know I wanted my Debbie to marry Robert. I told you what a fine young man he was. The fly in the ointment was Peter Nemo. So I thought if she would see that slob there wouldn't be any question—

DOCTOR I tried to dissuade you.

LIBBY I didn't listen. And the worst possible thing happened. She went off with him—to Nyack she went—and who knows what the consequences of that can be? Companionate marriage, it could be.

DOCTOR I know about this already, Mrs. Hirsch. Debbie called me from the bus station.

LIBBY What did she tell you?

DOCTOR You know it's confidential.

LIBBY Did she tell you I interfered with Robert and that woman?

DOCTOR In general, but I don't know the details.

LIBBY I called her up and I invited her to the wedding. I tried to be polite but I suppose I sounded like a—like a blackmailer.

DOCTOR Were you a successful blackmailer?

LIBBY A failure. She called Robert. Robert hollered at Debbie. He hollered at me. Suffice it to say, he slammed the door.

DOCTOR You've had quite a day.

LIBBY And also my husband left me.

DOCTOR Your husband left you? Why was that?

LIBBY I interfered in a business deal contrary to the way Paul wanted. . . . Right now he's negotiating for a one-bedroom house in Deland, Florida, for us. . . . What do I mean *us*? For *him*. For *them*. Selma Harris.

DOCTOR Who's Selma Harris?

LIBBY She worked for my husband for fifteen years. Mildred warned me. She was smarter than I am.

DOCTOR Why do you say that?

LIBBY Because she understood. She understood about Robert. She understood about Paul. . . . Now they're all gone—Mildred, too.

DOCTOR Yes?

LIBBY I called her David and I gave that a little push. . . . (*Looking at him*) Doctor, what did I do wrong? . . . People that I loved more than my life—like strangers—like I never knew them.

DEAR ME, THE SKY IS FALLING

DOCTOR   Lie back, Mrs. Hirsch. You'll be more comfortable.

LIBBY   (*Relaxing again*) Everything I wanted for them, they wanted something else.

DOCTOR   Are you sure of that, Mrs. Hirsch?

LIBBY   An empty house is a loud answer.

DOCTOR   How can I help?

LIBBY   The trouble is that I'm already figuring out what to do next . . . and I need your help to *stop* me from figuring out what to do next.

DOCTOR   (*Rising, and moving his chair so they can see each other*) Mrs. Hirsch, you're not my patient and I'm not going to talk to you as a doctor. I'm going to talk to you as a friend. Now— (*He sits*) Everything you wanted for your family was right.

LIBBY   But everything I did was wrong.

DOCTOR   It was intelligent of you to want Debbie to marry a decent, respectable man. It's immature of her to go off with that slob. I mean . . . what's his name?

LIBBY   Peter Nemo.

DOCTOR   Nemo. She doesn't want him. She just wants to show *you* that she's independent.

LIBBY   She's certainly showing me.

DOCTOR   As for your husband—instead of retiring, he needs to participate more. But he feels that his life is over with all his children married. About that you have true insight and you used leadership.

LIBBY   Some leadership. So what do I do now, Doctor?

DOCTOR   Don't rush me, Mrs. Hirsch. Your sister Mildred knows she made a mistake about David, but she will never give you the satisfaction of telling you. She prefers to see you squirm. And that's what they all want and need, Mrs. Hirsch—to see you squirm—because you are their yardstick. You are the one they seek to please or displease. They give or withhold their love, using it as a weapon. And you don't deserve that because your motives are unselfish.

LIBBY   I'm not unselfish. I'm the most selfish person in the world. Everything I wanted for them, I wanted for me. . . . So you see what happened? Everything is out with the ashes.

DOCTOR   It's time for the oil burner, Mrs. Hirsch. You get the same results in the end and maybe the house will be warmer.

LIBBY   There's nobody in the house.

DOCTOR   Well, I think there's a possibility they'll come back.

LIBBY   (*Looking at him—hopefully*)   You heard something?

DOCTOR   No. Only that there's no point in their behaving outrageously if *you* don't know about it. There's no sense in making a grandstand play if there's nobody in the grandstand. What you must do, Mrs. Hirsch, is be permissive.

LIBBY   What's permissive?

DOCTOR   Let them do as they wish—abdicate your leadership—and see what happens.

LIBBY   And if they *don't* come back? . . . Doctor, I have problems.

DOCTOR   Of course you have problems, Mrs. Hirsch. Some of them of your own making.

LIBBY   Don't I know it.

DOCTOR   But what you're facing is normal—the normal, everyday living of normal, everyday people.

LIBBY   This is normal? To be talking to you like this is normal?

DOCTOR   A doctor can be a friend.

LIBBY   A friend comes to your house and has supper and you talk. You don't go to a friend's office to talk.

DOCTOR   I'd be happy to come to your house for supper and talk.

LIBBY (*Looking at him*)   You mean it?

DOCTOR   Certainly.

LIBBY (*A wave of the hand*)   This is part of your treatment. You're trying to make me into a new woman. . . . The trouble is, what'll I do with the old one?

DOCTOR   Tell me, isn't there anything you want for Libby Hirsch? Not for her husband, or her children, or her house—just for Libby?

LIBBY   I have everything I want—or had.

DOCTOR   For *you*—Libby. Something for *you*.

LIBBY (*Shaking her head*)   Nothing.

DOCTOR   Oh, everybody has something deep in their hearts. Some unfulfilled dream. Some aborted hope.

LIBBY   You mean—all the way back? Before I was engaged? . . . If anybody would ask me, I would say I wish I could sing.

DOCTOR Why don't you?

LIBBY I haven't opened my mouth in years.

DOCTOR When was the last time?

LIBBY I sang in the Temple choir. Of course, not a solo—but I managed to keep on key. God gave me a small, natural voice.

DOCTOR Why don't you use it?

LIBBY Who would listen?

DOCTOR *You.*

LIBBY And would I play the piano for my own solo?

DOCTOR If you can.

LIBBY I can. Mama gave us all lessons. I used to play in the school auditorium. . . . Brahms, I played. . . . And how I enjoyed that. . . . I used to imagine John Barrymore was in the audience. . . .

DOCTOR (*Appreciatively*) John Barrymore?

LIBBY I had some crush on him! . . . All my life, when the bundle got heavy, I'd imagine John Barrymore was taking me on a magic carpet to Paris.

DOCTOR (*Gently*) Why Paris?

LIBBY Paris I dream about. . . . Paris in the spring. . . . April in Paris. . . . Chestnuts in blossom. . . . (*She hums a bit then, catching herself*) How'd I get to chestnuts?

DOCTOR You're free-associating.

LIBBY Is that psychoanalysis?

DOCTOR   Yes, it is.

LIBBY (*Looking at him piteously*)   Doctor dear? Do you
  think there's any hope for me?
  (*Unable to hold back her tears, she searches in her
  bag for a handkerchief. He hands her his*)

  Curtain

Act Three

ACT THREE

The scene: The Hirsch living room. Two hours later.

The rise: The card table is set up. JESSIE *is dealing to* MINNIE *and* SOPHIE. LIBBY *enters from the pantry, carrying a bowl of fruit, plates and napkins. She sets them on a coffee table near the card table.*

LIBBY Is it all right to put marinated steaks in the freezer?

SOPHIE Not if they were in the freezer before, Libby.

LIBBY I didn't take any chances. I ground up the meat and I'll have stuffed cabbage tomorrow. But for who?
(She sits at the card table. SOPHIE *rises and goes to the fruit bowl for a grape)*

MINNIE They'll all be back. I feel it in my bones.

JESSIE This whole thing will pass like it never happened.

SOPHIE I don't see any sense taking such an optimistic view. *(She goes back to her chair)* We're Libby's friends and we should advise her.

LIBBY If I need any advice, Sophie, I'm already getting it from a very good man.

SOPHIE All right—but at least call *somebody* up!

LIBBY Who?

MINNIE Mildred, at least.

JESSIE At least Mildred.

LIBBY (*She dials*)   There's no answer.

JESSIE   You think she went out with David?

LIBBY   I don't know who went out with who—or who's doing what. All I can do is sit and wait. If you want to wait with me, let's play cards.
(*The phone rings.* LIBBY *rises*)

SOPHIE   Oh, thank God, it's somebody!

JESSIE   Hurry! Answer!

MINNIE   They'll hang up!
(*The phone rings again*)

LIBBY   I don't want them to think I'm anxious! Let it ring three times! I don't want them to think I'm anxious. (*The phone rings the third time. She picks it up*) Hello? . . . Hello, Mrs. Schlinger. . . . (*The girls groan in disappointment*)   No, my husband is not here at the moment. . . . Yeah? Thirty-five-five? If you could stretch to thirty-six, maybe you'd have a deal. . . . Thirty-five seven-fifty. I guess that's all right. . . . I don't have to ask him. He's the one who wants to sell— and, besides, the property is in his wife's name. . . . When would you want to take possession? . . . Two weeks! Mrs. Schlinger, please, how can I clear out a lifetime's accumulation in two weeks? . . . Well, at least a month. . . . All right, let's say it's a deal subject to the terms you suggest. . . . Well, I hope you'll be happy here. I was—very. Goodbye. (*She hangs up*)   I think that's a very nice price for this house.

JESSIE   I feel like crying!

MINNIE   It's a bitter blow to the neighborhood!

SOPHIE   I think you could have gotten five hundred more if you held out.

LIBBY What have I got to hold out for? How long can I rattle around in ten rooms all by myself.

MINNIE It won't be by yourself.

JESSIE They'll be back.

LIBBY Let's play cards.

MINNIE (*Rising*) This whole thing is making me so nervous! And you know me, girls, when I get nervous— (*She raises her hand as though for permission*) May I leave the room, please?
  (*She hurries upstairs*)

LIBBY (*Listening*) Do I hear somebody?

JESSIE Two people are walking up the porch!

LIBBY Make believe we don't see them! Play cards— three-handed. (*They play furiously.* DEBBIE *enters, closing the door behind her*) Hello, Debbie. Did you have a nice time in Nyack?

DEBBIE No, Mama, I didn't.

LIBBY Oh, I'm sorry.

SOPHIE Hello, Debbie darling!

DEBBIE Hello, Aunt Sophie—Aunt Jessie.

JESSIE Hello, dear.

SOPHIE Such a lovely day. I'm surprised you didn't have a good time.

JESSIE I love to go to the country in the spring.

SOPHIE Especially around Nyack!

DEBBIE Everybody loves to go to the country in the spring —especially around Nyack. . . . I've just come back to pick up a few things.

LIBBY (*Still looking at her cards*) Good, darling. Has Aunt Mildred room for you?

DEBBIE No, Mama. I've made other plans.

LIBBY I'm sure you have very good reasons.

SOPHIE (*Looking*) Her other plans are standing on the porch, Libby. That Peter Nemo.

LIBBY Sophie, don't interfere.

DEBBIE Peter and I are going to see if we can find some kind of fulfillment together.

LIBBY If that's what you want, I hope you'll be happy.

DEBBIE But, Mama! We are not thinking in terms of the Hampshire House and mock turtle soup!

LIBBY (*Not turning*) Why should you, darling? Are you thinking of eloping to Maryland?

DEBBIE No, Mama!

LIBBY Maybe downtown New York with a judge?

DEBBIE No, Mama.

LIBBY Maybe Philadelphia with Peter's mother?

DEBBIE No, Mama! Nowhere! Peter's a free soul.

LIBBY (*Still looking at her cards*) Well, I'm in no position to argue. All I can say is, if that's what you really want . . .

DEBBIE It's what I *really* want.

LIBBY It's your life, darling, and I'm glad to see you're showing some leadership. I'm sure Dr. Evans will be very happy. Incidentally, would you mind if I take from him, too?

DEBBIE   You, Mama? You in psychoanalysis?

LIBBY   Why not? It was quite a relief this afternoon to make a transference.

DEBBIE   This afternoon?

LIBBY   Yes. I had another session with Dr. Evans. So don't you worry about me, darling. Just worry about yourself.

MINNIE (*Coming downstairs*)   Hello, Debbie darling! Did you have a nice time in Nyack?

DEBBIE (*Snapping*)   Yes!

LIBBY   Do you want me to help you pack?

DEBBIE   Pack what, Mama?

LIBBY   You said you wanted to pick up a few things. Does he have enough closet space?

DEBBIE   I don't know. (*Then, angrily*)   Where is my camp duffle bag?

LIBBY   Upstairs in the attic, where you put it.

DEBBIE   I didn't put it, Mama. *You* put it.

LIBBY   At least the doctor accomplished one thing. I'll never put again.

DEBBIE (*Furious*)   I don't know what you're up to, Mama, but your tricks just won't work any more!
    (*She rushes up the stairs*)

MINNIE   For goodness' sake! What happened, for goodness' sake?

SOPHIE (*Gesturing* MINNIE *to be quiet*)   Later! (MINNIE *sits at the card table*)   Are you just going to sit there, Libby, and let her do this terrible thing?

DEAR ME, THE SKY IS FALLING

LIBBY   I have to be permissive.

SOPHIE   There's a limit! It's a sin!

JESSIE   You're going too far!

LIBBY   I'm trying to be the new woman. It's not easy, but I'm trying. . . . She was a little disappointed when I didn't fight with her, huh?

SOPHIE   Yes.

LIBBY   She expected me to tell her what *not* to do.

SOPHIE   You always have.

LIBBY   From now on, she'll tell herself. If it kills me, she'll tell herself. (*Listening*)   There's Paul. . . . Listen how he's driving that car.

MINNIE   Have you got an attack of mental telepathy?

LIBBY   He's had a highball already—maybe two. . . . Now he's at the back door. (*Starting for the stairs*)   I'll get the Sal Hepatica. (*Stops*)   I mustn't interfere. . . . He's in the kitchen. (*She hurries to sit in her chair at the card table*)   Play cards! (PAUL *enters from the pantry, wearing his golf cap and carrying his golf bag. He puts the bag in the sunroom*)   The girls just dropped in for a little canasta, Paul.

GIRLS   (*Overly-enthusiastically*)   Hello, Paul! You look marvelous! So glad to see you!

PAUL   (*Turning from setting down the golf bag*)   What's the matter—you're all so glad to see me?

LIBBY   The girls are always glad to see you, Paul.

PAUL   Yeah. Only this time they're a little more enthusiastic. Debbie home?

LIBBY   Yes.

PAUL   That's a relief. Well, *I'm* home, too. Where's the Sal Hepatica?

LIBBY   (*Rising automatically*)   You want me to get it for you?

PAUL   Just tell me where it is.

LIBBY   It's upstairs in the medicine chest.

PAUL   I—had a few drinks.

LIBBY   Why not?

PAUL   (*Surprised*)   You know I shouldn't drink with my diverticulitis.

LIBBY   What harm can it do now and then?

PAUL   (*Proudly*)   I was celebrating.

LIBBY   Oh?

PAUL   Don't you want to know what?

LIBBY   If you want to tell me, you'll tell me.

PAUL   I made a hole-in-one!

LIBBY   A whole hole-in-one?

PAUL   On the fifth hole! The one with the gully! I didn't believe it myself until Aaron Bender said, "Look, your pill's in the cup," and I said, "That's not my ball. That's Joe Weldon's." And Joe said, "No, it's yours, Paul! It's an honest-to-God hole-in-one!"
        (*He brings forth the ball from his jacket pocket, tosses it in the air and catches it*)

LIBBY   Congratulations.
        (*The girls ad lib "Isn't that nice," etc.*)

PAUL   (*Happily*)   So we went back to the nineteenth

hole and we had a few drinks! Everybody made a big fuss and I got a hole-in-one pin from the president of the club!

(*He shows* LIBBY *his lapel*)

LIBBY It looks very nice.
(*She sits and picks up her cards*)

PAUL Very nice? Is that all you can say? You know how many people ever made a hole-in-one? It's only the second time in thirty-two years anybody ever made a hole-in-one on that fifth hole! Libby, that's the one with the gully! They're giving me a cup at the annual founder's dinner.

LIBBY (*Looking at her cards*) Very nice.

PAUL Very nice. You already said that! That's all you can say?

LIBBY I'm so excited, I'm speechless.

PAUL (*Deflated*) I don't think so. (*Starting upstairs*) Where's Debbie?

LIBBY In the attic.

PAUL (*Stops*) In the attic? What's she doing up there?

LIBBY Looking for her duffle bag.

PAUL Why?

LIBBY I think she can explain it better herself.

PAUL (*As he goes up and out of sight*) It can't be anything serious. Not with your head on canasta.

SOPHIE You want us to go, Libby?

LIBBY Please, girls.
(*The girls rise and prepare to leave*)

MINNIE   We understand, Libby.

JESSIE   He looks very tired.

LIBBY   It's not easy to make a hole-in-one.
(*The phone rings.* LIBBY *hurries to it, but is waiting for the third ring*)

SOPHIE (*As she goes out the door*)   If you want us for anything, Libby, just call up.
(*The phone rings*)

JESSIE   Don't be too permissive, Libby!

MINNIE (*Following them*)   Freud should only drop dead!
(*The phone rings.* MINNIE *closes the door.* LIBBY *picks up the phone*)

LIBBY   Hello. . . . Chicago? Yes, put her on, please. . . . Hello, Clara. Are the children all right? . . . Oh? Papa called to tell you about the hole-in-one, huh? Wasn't that wonderful? . . . Well, what can I tell you, Clara? We had a crisis here concerning Debbie and Robert. . . . Don't make any plans to come to the wedding because there won't be any. . . . And don't call Robert. . . . No, there's no point in coming. (PAUL *comes downstairs.* LIBBY'S *back is to him*) No, just call Louise. . . . Oh, you did? And Teddy, too? . . . Yes, Papa's home.

PAUL   I'm here.
(*He takes the phone*)

LIBBY   It's Clara. She wants to talk to you.

PAUL   Hello, Clara. (*He picks up the phone base and moves away from* LIBBY *a bit, facing into the dining room*) Um hmmm . . . Um hmm . . . Hm umm . . . Yes . . . Well . . . Please, Clara, please stop giving me

93

instructions. You sound more like your mother every day. (*He looks at* LIBBY) So hang up already. It's practically three minutes. . . . My love to Adrian and the kids. . . . Just a minute. (*Holding out the phone to* LIBBY) Anything else you want to say to her?

LIBBY (*Speaking loudly*)   All my love and a big kiss.

PAUL   Goodbye, Clara.
(*He hangs up and sets the phone back on the bench*)

LIBBY   It was very nice of you to call Clara and tell her about the hole-in-one.

PAUL   I wanted to tell somebody.

LIBBY   Why didn't you call me and tell me?

PAUL   We weren't on such good terms when I left this morning.

LIBBY   For that, I apologize—and for many, many other things.

PAUL   This is Dr. Evans talking? (*He holds her eyes for a moment*)   I know. Debbie told me.

LIBBY   I went, and I'm going to go again—not regularly, but whenever I have a problem.

PAUL   You have a problem now. You have a daughter going away with that person standing on the porch.

LIBBY   It's her life.

PAUL   Did the analyst tell you what to do about that?

LIBBY   He says to do nothing.

PAUL   He thinks that's good?

LIBBY   It's what *she* thinks is good.

PAUL Well, I don't think it's good! . . . All right, maybe I should have stopped her earlier, but an afternoon in Nyack is one thing. A lifetime is something else.

LIBBY And with you one afternoon is all right?

PAUL No. But I force myself to say she's an adult and she has a right.

LIBBY So I am also forcing myself.

PAUL Libby, we have to do something!

LIBBY Paul—mature adults must act like mature adults. That's a new law that was passed in this house.
(*He disappears into the dining room. She goes to the piano, looks after him, then sits and begins to play—slowly and not too skillfully—Mozart's "Sonata in C"*)

PAUL (*Re-entering, stunned, not believing his ears*) Why are you playing the piano suddenly?

LIBBY Because I feel like it—and the modern thing is to do what you feel like. Be permissive with yourself.

PAUL Stop being so permissive and listen.

LIBBY And if I listen, what'll I hear? That you're going to Florida without me? That you're selling your business? . . . *You're* being permissive. . . . And if it's all right for you, it's all right for me.

PAUL Debbie's more important than Florida. I'm putting Florida out of my mind until we settle this thing with Debbie. . . . Also with Aaron Bender. Don't you want to know what's with Aaron Bender?

LIBBY If you want to tell me. . . .

PAUL He says my buying out Charlie Finkel is a mar-

velous proposition and he's willing to back me entirely
on my reputation!

LIBBY   Very nice.

PAUL   Very nice? It's a great tribute!

LIBBY   What do you need, headaches? After all these
years, like you said yourself, you're entitled to play golf
breakfast, dinner and supper.

PAUL   And like *you* said, it's worth discussing.

LIBBY   We have thirty days to discuss.

PAUL   What thirty days?

LIBBY   When they take possession.

PAUL   When who takes possession?

LIBBY   The Schlingers.

PAUL   Who Schlingers? What Schlingers?

LIBBY   *Your* Schlingers. I sold them the house.

PAUL   You sold them what house?

LIBBY   This house.

PAUL (*Shouting*)   You sold *my* house?

LIBBY   It's in my name.

PAUL   That's a legal fiction!

LIBBY   The non-fiction is you can go to Florida.

PAUL   Will you stop playing the piano?

LIBBY   And if you go to Florida, I'm going to Paris.
            (PAUL *turns, stunned, as she segues into Puccini's*
            "Musetta's Waltz" from La Boheme)

PAUL What Paris? Who Paris?

LIBBY Same old Paris—and I'm taking singing lessons. (*She sings*)

PAUL Libby—you know, you are going crazy. (*The phone rings*)

LIBBY Telephone, darling.

PAUL (*Mimics*) "Telephone, darling." (*The phone rings again. He answers it*) Hello? . . . Who in Los Angeles? . . . Oh, Louise . . . (*To* LIBBY) Will you stop that piano?

LIBBY It's like riding a bicycle. You never forget.

PAUL You never rode a bicycle!

LIBBY On three wheels I rode.

MILDRED'S VOICE (*From outside the house*) Will you please excuse me, I'd like to go in the door!
(*She opens the door and enters*)

PETER (*Just outside the door*) Will you tell Debbie I'm growing fungus waiting out here?

MILDRED (*Closes the door*) Libby! I've got to talk to you!

PAUL Mildred, will you please stop shouting? It's Louise from Los Angeles. . . . Hello, Louise. . . . No, it's not TV. It's your mother playing—

MILDRED Libby, it's a matter of life and death! (LIBBY *stops playing*) Do you know what he wanted? To tell me that he wants a divorce because he's contemplating marrying a widow!!

LIBBY At least, now you know it's over. You know where you stand and you can adjust.
(*She begins Beethoven's "Minuet in G"*)

MILDRED I don't want to adjust! You stirred it up, Libby, you've got to do something.

LIBBY I don't stop anything any more or start it.

PAUL (*Into the phone*) Louise, I don't think so. Wait a minute. I'll ask your mother. (*He shouts to* LIBBY) Libby, Louise wants to take the first plane. She thinks she can talk some sense into Debbie. She says they were always very close. . . .
    (DEBBIE *appears on the stairs, carrying her duffle bag*)

LIBBY Oh, no, they weren't! (*She stops playing*) You always preferred Debbie and don't think Louise didn't know it. She was very jealous. I always had to give her more love and bigger pieces of cake.
    (*She begins playing, repeating the "Minuet in G"*)

PAUL Louise, I'll have to call you back. Love to everybody.

LIBBY Send mine also.

MILDRED And mine.

DEBBIE And mine.
    (*Setting down her duffle bag*)

PAUL The whole family sends likewise.
    (*He hangs up*)

DEBBIE Mama—what do you mean Louise was always jealous of me?

LIBBY And Clara was jealous of Louise. It happens to all sisters.

MILDRED I was never jealous of you.

LIBBY (*Stops playing*) Oh, yes, you were, darling. You were jealous because I had a family. And I was jealous of you because you got the highest marks, and you were so intellectual, and you had such a beautiful figure.

MILDRED   A lot of good it did me! You got all the boys.

LIBBY   Yeah? So who got Albert from Richmond Hill? (*She plays the "Black Bottom"*)

MILDRED   Albert from Richmond Hill? (*Remembering*) That skinny-marink with the red hair? (*She begins to move to the music*)

LIBBY   Ohh, he had some crush on you! . . . Remember? (MILDRED *dances for a moment; then*)

MILDRED   We really had fun in those days—you and I really had some fun! (*She hugs* LIBBY *happily*)

PAUL   Will you stop reminiscing? And will you stop playing that piano? (LIBBY *segues to "Tea For Two." To* DEBBIE) Do you know what your mother did? She sold this house. We've got to get out in thirty days—

DEBBIE   Thirty days? Mama, what am I going to do with my books and my record collection? Mama! Will you *please* stop playing the piano?

MILDRED   Libby, darling, David adores you. Why don't you call him up and tell him he's making a mistake.

DEBBIE   Aunt Mildred, can't you see we have a crisis around here?

MILDRED   And who caused it? You! You caused it! Your poor mother drives herself crazy to find you a little happiness in this world and who's standing out there on the porch? A fine, upstanding lawyer? No! A bum!

LIBBY   (*To* DEBBIE *as she stops playing*)   Darling, if you're taking such an important step with that gentleman, at least ask him to come in.

PAUL   Don't do it, Debbie! I don't want him in this house.

LIBBY   Paul, you told her to find herself.
  (DEBBIE *opens the door.* PETER *steps inside*)

PAUL   Well, I don't like what she found! (LIBBY *begins the "Golden Wedding" by Gilbrait. To* DEBBIE) So this is the gentleman you're going to spend the rest of your life with?

LIBBY   He's a free soul.

PETER   Why, thank you, Mrs. Hirsch.

PAUL   Free? What's such a holiday with being free? Debbie, a woman needs security and love and a husband!

PETER   A woman needs a man!

LIBBY   You said it!

PETER   Debbie and I don't need any legal mumbo-jumbo.

PAUL   Debbie, did we raise you to ruin yourself? (LIBBY *stops playing*) Did we educate you and love you to hand you over to an irresponsible nothing?

PETER   You'd have called Eugene O'Neill an irresponsible nothing.

LIBBY   A girl has to learn about life some time. She has to grow up.

MILDRED   She also has to live in the world. You can't defy conventions!

LIBBY   You don't understand young people these days. To them marriage is archaic. (*She starts to play "Poor Butterfly"*) Maybe we'd have had a better life, too, if *we* hadn't been tied by artificial mumbo-jumbo.

PAUL   We had a marvelous life! And stop the music!
(*He takes her hands from the keys and closes the piano*)

LIBBY   Did we, Paul? Did we have such a marvelous life?

PAUL   If that remark is a reference to a certain party—

LIBBY (*Quieting him*)   Please, Paul!

MILDRED (*To* DEBBIE, *taking her hand*)   Debbie—next to your mother, David likes you the best in the family. Why don't you call him up for me?

DEBBIE (*Looking at* LIBBY)   Mama should call him!

PAUL (*To* LIBBY)   Mama should call the Schlingers!

LIBBY (*Rising and moving to the stairs*)   No. Mama is not calling—not calling the Schlingers, not calling David. I'm not sitting in the grandstand any more, because in me you see a woman who is no longer an interfering wife, mother or sister. (*She turns back*)   Oh, Peter! I hope we see you often because you'll be almost a son-in-law!
(*As they stare, she goes upstairs.* PAUL *sinks onto the piano bench. Dazed,* DEBBIE *sits on the sofa and* MILDRED *sits in the armchair*)

PETER (*Looks at them, rises suddenly*)   Whoof! Debbie, let's split, please, before I get strangled by your umbilical cord!
(*The phone rings.* PAUL *rises*)

MILDRED   Maybe it's David!

PAUL   Maybe it's the Schlingers!

PETER   Maybe it's the wrong number!
(*The phone rings again*)

PAUL (*Picking up the phone*) Hello? Los Alamos. It's Teddy. Hello, Teddy. . . . So you talked to Clara and Louise. . . . What's the trouble?! Freud! Your mother is suffering from an overdose of Freud! . . . You're so smart you're telling *me* to do something? But how can I do something if I'm talking to you?

MILDRED Send my love.

DEBBIE Mine, too.

PETER Mine, too.

PAUL (*Glares at* PETER) Love from everybody here . . . to everybody there. Goodbye, Teddy.
  (*He hangs up and starts upstairs*)

DEBBIE Where are you going, Papa?

PAUL I'm going upstairs to talk to your mother to see if I at least have a roof over my head.
  (*He goes*)

MILDRED Debbie, *what* am I going to do? I'm so miserable.

DEBBIE Darling, what you need is to be alone. (*Starts her upstairs*) Now, go upstairs to my room and lie down on my chaise and just rest. Then you'll decide what you want to do—and whatever it is, darling, we'll all help you.

MILDRED (*Disappearing up the stairs*) Debbie, that's just what I wanted to hear.

DEBBIE (*Calling after her*) And maybe I'll come up and rub the back of your neck.

PETER I may be sick. . . . Debbie, I pulled you out of this exurbanite slime but you are slipping right back into it.

DEBBIE   Peter, she needed a little sympathy and warmth.

PETER   She's beyond saving.

DEBBIE (*Heatedly*)   She is my aunt and I love her!

PETER   You are addicted to her. You are acting out a fetal need in Westchester County that began on the shores of the Red Sea.

DEBBIE   And on the shores of the Hudson, *you* got on the bus first! *You* let *me* walk behind you! Your hill turned out to be a picnic ground for a boy scout troop! And now you're trying to crunch me by attacking everything I've ever lived with or loved! Ohh, I have some insight into you, Peter Nemo! Don't forget, I am in analysis!

PETER   Stop stalling and let's get out of here, please. (*Rising*)   Where's my mobile? (*He sees it on the dining room table*)   Oh.
    (*He goes into the dining room as the doorbell rings.* DEBBIE *answers*)

DEBBIE (*Stepping back—surprised*)   Hello.

ROBERT (*Stepping inside and closing the door*)   Debbie, I didn't know whether you'd be here or not. I'm glad you are. I'm a rational human being and I dislike myself when I act out of anger or emotion so, if you're not too intense, maybe we can sit down and talk sanely and find out where we are—and *if* we are. And, Debbie, I *hope* we are, because I need you.

PETER (*Coming from the dining room, carrying the A&P box*)   Hi-Ho, old daddy. You're too late. The earth has taken another spin. Say goodbye to the nice man, Debbie.

ROBERT   Has the earth taken another spin, Debbie?

DEBBIE (*Confused*) You're both crushing me and I don't know what to do.

PETER It's time to decide, baby.

ROBERT (*To him*) We finally agree.

DEBBIE I don't care whether you agree or not, Robert.

ROBERT (*Pauses; then, happily*) You remembered my name.

DEBBIE I did, didn't I?

ROBERT (*Eagerly*) What's my second name?

DEBBIE It's Wolfe! Robert Wolfe!

ROBERT Oh, Debbie! Look—I'll try very hard to let life wash over me in great waves! I'll do it your way!

DEBBIE Wait, Robert! Wait!

PETER You know, I feel like I'm looking at the Late Late Show! She's Joan Crawford and you're Clark Gable! No, *I'm* Clark Gable and you are Warner Baxter! . . . There's only one thing, Debbie—all those pictures have happy endings. And today, happy endings are in limbo.

DEBBIE I'm afraid you're in limbo, too, Peter. Oh, Robert—
   (*She moves into* ROBERT'S *arms*)

PETER (*Calling towards the stairs*) Mrs. Hirsch! Mom! Mama! (*To* DEBBIE *and* ROBERT) Excuse me. (*He goes to the foot of the stairs and calls up*) Oh, Mother! Mama! Mama! Mama! Mama! Pick up the chips! You're a big winner! (*He goes to the front door, picking up his A&P box as he says to* DEBBIE *and* ROBERT) And, you know, I am a winner, too. You are so deeply infected with the mama-virus, Debbie, that I would have succumbed eventually, too. (*He opens the door*) Okay. I hope you have a lot of children. But you better make reservations with a good analyst *now* because those kids don't have a moment to lose.

(*He goes.* ROBERT *closes the door behind him*)

DEBBIE   It can't be normal for me to be bobbing around like an emotional ping pong ball. I really ought to call my analyst.

ROBERT (*Holding out his arms*)   You better do your free-associating right here.

(*She moves into his arms. After a moment,* LIBBY *starts downstairs*)

LIBBY   Did I hear somebody call me?

DEBBIE (*Turning—happily*)   Peter, Mama. He's gone.

LIBBY (*Coming on down*)   Oh? I'm sorry I didn't have a chance to say goodbye. (*The back doorbell rings. She starts to the pantry door*) That's the back door. I'll get it.

DEBBIE   I'll go!

LIBBY (*At the door*)   No, no. I'm expecting somebody.

ROBERT   Mrs. Hirsch! Hello!

LIBBY (*With great formality*)   How do you do?
(*She goes into the pantry*)

DEBBIE (*Looks after her*)   I wonder why she's acting like this?

ROBERT   That was not a typical reaction.

DEBBIE   It must be something Dr. Evans said to her.

PAUL (*Coming downstairs*)   What was Peter shouting just now? I was on the phone— (*Seeing* ROBERT)

You're back, Robert?! You and Debbie together? Let's hurry quick and tell Mama.

DEBBIE She knows.

PAUL She knows? She must be out of her mind with satisfaction.

DEBBIE No, Papa.

PAUL Oh, you're having trouble, too? I told her I called the Schlingers and they let me out of the deal—and you think she was pleased? (LIBBY *comes from the pantry and starts for the stairs.* PAUL *tries to stop her*) Please—will you stay in one place?

LIBBY I have to comfort Mildred. She called David and he really wants a divorce.

PAUL At least that's settled.

DEBBIE Mama, what about us?

PAUL Aren't you glad the storm is over?

LIBBY Over? I still hear thunder.

MILDRED (*Coming downstairs*) It's time I went home. (*Seeing* ROBERT) When did Robert come back?

DEBBIE I'm awfully sorry about Uncle David, Aunt Mildred.

MILDRED So I'll go to Reno. And I won't waste my time. I'll study and, in the fall, I'll take examinations for principal. You know, Debbie, Dr. Evans was right! Instead of being depressed, I'm elated!

PAUL Libby? Aren't you elated? You can have what you want! You can send your invitations! You can have your wedding!

MILDRED Congratulations, Libby!

LIBBY   Believe me, this is no time for congratulations. Anybody who would give up a man like Robert at twelve o'clock, go away with a man like Peter at five minutes after twelve—

DEBBIE   But, Mama, I had an emotional crisis and I've come through it.

ROBERT   We both have.

PAUL   I say ditto.

MILDRED   I also say ditto.

LIBBY   Me, I don't say ditto.

DEBBIE   But it's exactly the way you planned it!

ROBERT   Exactly the way you and *my* mother planned it!

MILDRED   Ever since you first laid eyes on Robert—

PAUL   It was love at first sight!

LIBBY   Debbie, you are going to walk down the aisle on Papa's arm just to please me? No, thank you, Debbie. Better go find yourself an apartment—write that book— but make sure the girl in it really loves her husband.

ROBERT   Oh, no! Mrs. Hirsch, you're letting go, and I'm taking over!

LIBBY   Robert, don't be my replacement.

DEBBIE   Replacement! Mama, two sessions with Dr. Evans and you're the world's authority on psychoanalysis!

LIBBY   You see, darling? You *are* hostile to me.

ROBERT   Your mother makes sense, Debbie.

DEBBIE   How would *you* know? You reject psychotherapy!

ROBERT   Here we go again! Debbie, I refuse to submit to

this public examination of our love life. I'd like for once a little normal behavior between us! (*He goes to the front door*) So I'm off to have a hamburger—with everything! (*He opens the door and turns*) Delighted to buy you one. I'll be in the car, and you've got exactly two minutes. Goodnight, everybody.

(*He goes.* DEBBIE *takes a step after him, stops, then*)

PAUL   Debbie, I think you could use a cup of coffee.

MILDRED   Debbie, go after him or you'll be as big a dumb-bell as I.

DEBBIE   How do you counsel, Ma?

LIBBY   You're old enough to follow your own heart. I mean—your underlying psychic mechanism.

DEBBIE   (*Happily*) Well, I don't suppose a hamburger would do any harm! I love you, Mama!

LIBBY   And I love you.

DEBBIE   (*Smiling*) But that doesn't mean the Hampshire House!

(*She goes*)

PAUL   It's beginning to sound like our family.

MILDRED   At least I know where I am! Good night, Libby.

LIBBY   Good night, darling.

MILDRED   (*Kisses her*) I want to thank you—well, for being such a dear sibling! You, too, Paul!

(*She goes out the front door*)

LIBBY   So we're both siblings! Paul, take Mildred home. It's late. Drive her.

PAUL   All right, but first I have to talk to you about something. (*Goes to door and calls*) Mildred, wait! I'll take

you home in a minute. (*He comes back to* LIBBY)
Libby—

LIBBY   Paul, there's something on my mind, too. Why did
Clara, Louise and Teddy move so far away?

PAUL   Business.

LIBBY   Business? Or to get away from me?

PAUL   Don't be ridiculous. Don't they call you whenever
they have a problem? Who do they turn to?

LIBBY   They turn. But long distance. Maybe it'll be better for Debbie, too—long distance. So, Paul, sell the
house and let's move to Florida.

PAUL   No. I can't get out of my mind what Aaron
Bender said about my buying out Charlie Finkel. He
said it was a good proposition.

LIBBY   Well, if I were an interfering wife, I would say,
merge with Finkel and you run the business for six
months—and let Charlie run it for six months. But, of
course, I'm no longer an interfering wife.

PAUL   How do you like that! It's just what I had in mind.
But, Libby, there's something else—

LIBBY   Mildred is waiting, Paul.

PAUL   There's something else—something more important.

LIBBY   All right, Paul. Say it. Say Selma Harris.

PAUL   Libby, I don't know what you heard, but I give you
my word—

LIBBY   You gave me your word May twelfth, nineteen
twenty-six, Paul. Once was enough.

PAUL   Libby, I swear to you—

LIBBY   You don't have to. Who knows you better than I do? (*Their foreheads touch for a moment*) Now, take Mildred home. Go, Mildred's waiting. (*He heads for the pantry door*) Go the front way!

PAUL   Why?

LIBBY   Because I have another man hidden in the kitchen!

PAUL   Give him my regards!
(*He goes out the front door.* LIBBY *opens the pantry door to admit* DR. EVANS. *He carries his hat*)

LIBBY   You came just on time, Doctor.

DOCTOR   I'm very punctual.

LIBBY   Please excuse me for asking you to come through the back way but I didn't want you to bump into the family.

DOCTOR   And it *is* your family again, isn't it?

LIBBY   You heard?

DOCTOR   I heard.

LIBBY   Did I say everything right? Did I do everything right?

DOCTOR   You were effective and reasonable and your family responded in kind.

LIBBY   Thanks to you.

DOCTOR   (*Looking the room over*) Ah, yes. I should have known your home would reflect you.
(*He places his hat on the piano bench*)

DEAR ME, THE SKY IS FALLING

LIBBY   Some old furniture and worn-out carpets.

DOCTOR   It's the kind of house I've always dreamed of living in.

LIBBY   Your unfulfilled dream? Why don't you buy one? (*Indicating with her hand that he should sit on the sofa*) There are many for sale in this neighborhood.

DOCTOR   My wife prefers an apartment.
         (*As he sits*)

LIBBY   Yeah, but if *you* like a house?

DOCTOR   We both agree it would be too much for her.

LIBBY   She doesn't like housekeeping?

DOCTOR   She's an excellent housekeeper, Mrs. Hirsch. She's also an excellent psychoanalyst.

LIBBY   The both of you?

DOCTOR   The both of us.

LIBBY   Do you analyze each other?

DOCTOR (*Laughs*)   Oh, no, Mrs. Hirsch. No, we just love each other.

LIBBY   Just like everybody else.

DOCTOR (*Wearily—pinching the bridge of his nose*)   Just like everybody else.

LIBBY   You look tired. You know what you need? You need a vacation; that's what you need.

DOCTOR (*Smiling*)   Now don't you try to be a temporary mother substitute.

LIBBY Why temporary? I'm available to be a mother on a full-time basis. . . . Why don't you lie down on the couch, Doctor?

    (*The curtain starts down slowly as she plumps the pillows and urges him to lie down. He smilingly demurs. He is still successfully protesting as*)

Curtain